gold **nuggets**

Messages from Existence

ALL YOU HAVE IS THIS VERY MOMENT, DO NOT GO ON POSTPONING

The material in this book is selected from various talks by Osho given to a live audience.
All of Osho's talks have been published in full as books, and are also available as original audio recordings.
Audio recordings and the complete text archive can be found via the online OSHO Library at www.osho.com

OSHO is a registered trademark of OSHO International Foundation, www.osho.com/trademarks

OSHO MEDIA INTERNATIONAL

New York • London • Mumbai

an imprint of
OSHO INTERNATIONAL
www.osho.com/oshointernational

Distributed by Publishers Group Worldwide
www.pgw.com

Library of Congress Cataloging-in-Publication Data is available

ISBN 13: 978-0-9818341-3-9
ISBN 10: 0-9818341-3-2

Printed in India

10 9 8 7 6 5 4 3 2 1

Design by Terry Jeavons
Copyright on Osho-image on jacket: © OSHO International Foundation

EXISTENCE AND YOU ARE ENOUGH. There is no need for any agent between you and existence to interpret, to say, "How beautiful!" to take messages from you to existence and bring messages from existence to you.

In the East it is said that the universe is like a spider's web. If you touch a single thread of the spider's web, the whole web will feel the vibration. Touch a single blade of grass and you have touched the greatest star, the farthest away star, because the whole is an organic unity; nothing is unrelated. It is only human ignorance that has created the idea of the ego.

And man lives in a kind of self-exile; it is self-imposed exile. We have made a small capsule around ourselves; we have become encapsulated, alienated. And then we suffer, then we are miserable. Then we can't find any meaning in life, any significance in life. Then we feel uprooted, ungrounded. Then we feel accidental, as if we are not needed at all, as if existence would go on running in the same way whether we are or we are not. That gives us a deep wound. We lose confidence, trust in ourselves. We become something futile, unneeded, useless; just by accident we have come into existence.

And this whole nonsense arises because we have created the idea of the ego. The ego is an effort to disconnect yourself from the whole, although you cannot disconnect yourself from whole, but you can live in the belief that you have succeeded. Your belief is the cause of your hell. Drop the belief of the ego and suddenly you will see messengers running between you and the whole continuously, every moment, day in, day out. Then the birds singing bring messages, the flowers opening bring messages, then the stars twinkling in the night bring messages. Then the whole existence becomes an open book, the real Bible. Then you need not go into old, rotten scriptures; you can simply look around and start reading existence. And then there are sermons everywhere, scriptures everywhere, songs everywhere.

With existence you have to be silent; all talking should stop. You are not to say something. On the contrary, a prayer is a listening. You have to listen to existence, not to say something. If you speak, who will listen? If you talk and you are too involved in the words, then who will listen? And every moment there is a message.

Live totally, and live intensely, so that each moment becomes golden and your whole life becomes a series of golden moments.

Such a person never dies because he has the Midas touch: Whatever he touches becomes golden.

This small life that you have got can be turned into a paradise. This very earth is the lotus paradise.

The only authentic responsibility is towards your own potential, your intelligence and awareness and to act accordingly.

With birth you are not born as a tree, you are born only as a seed. You have to grow to the point where you come to a flowering, and that flowering will be your contentment, fulfillment.

This flowering has nothing to do with power, nothing to do with money, nothing to do with politics. It has something to do absolutely with you; it is an individual progress.

You have to become a celebration unto yourself.

The yearning for a utopia is basically the yearning for harmony in the individual and in the society. The harmony has never existed: there has always been chaos. Society has been divided into different cultures, different religions, different nations – and all based on superstitions. None of the divisions are valid. But these divisions show that man is divided within himself. These are the projections of his own inner conflict. He is not one within, that's why he could not create one society, one humanity, outside.

The cause is not outside.

The outside is only the reflection of the inner man.

Nobody has paid much attention to the individual. And that is the root cause of all the problems.

But because the individual seems to be so small, and the society seems so big, people think that we can change society and then the individuals will change. This is not going to be so because 'society' is only a word; there are only individuals, there is no society. The society has no soul; you cannot change anything in it. You can change only the individual, howsoever small he appears. And once you know the science of how to change the individual it is applicable to all the individuals everywhere.

My feeling is that one day we are going to attain a society which will be harmonious, which will be far better than all the ideas that utopians have been producing for thousands of years.

You are never quite satisfied with who you are and with what existence has given you because you have been distracted. You have been directed where nature has not meant you to be. You are not moving towards your own potential.

What others wanted you to be, you are trying to be, but it cannot be satisfying. When it is not satisfying, logic says, 'Perhaps it is not enough – have more of it.' Then you go after more, then you start looking around.

And everybody is appearing with a mask which is smiling, happy-looking, so everybody is deceiving everybody else. You also appear with a mask, so others think you are happier; you think others are happier. The grass looks greener on the other side of the fence. They see your grass and it looks greener. It really looks greener, thicker, better. That is the illusion that distance creates.

When you come close, then you start seeing that it is not so. But people keep each other at a distance. Even friends, even lovers, keep each other at a distance; too much closeness will be dangerous, they may see your reality. And you have been misguided from the very beginning, so whatever you do will remain miserable. You see somebody with much money: you think perhaps money brings joy. Look at that person, how joyous he seems to be. So run after money. Somebody is healthier run after health. Somebody is doing something else and looks very contented follow him. But it is always the others.

The society has managed it so that you will never think about your own potential. And the whole misery is that you are not being yourself. Just be yourself, and then there is no misery and no competition and no botheration that others have more, that you don't have more.

If you like grass to be greener, there is no need to look on the other side of the fence; make the grass greener on your side of the fence. It is such a simple thing to make the grass greener.

Man has to be rooted in his own potential, whatever it is. And the world will be so contented that you cannot believe it.

To be alive means to have a sense of humor, to have a deep, loving quality, to have playfulness.

I am absolutely against all life-negative attitudes; and respect for the divine has been life-negative. To make it life-affirmative, playfulness, a sense of humor, love and respect, have all to be joined together.

Reverence for life is the only respect for the divine, because there is nothing more divine than life itself.

Man is born with great treasures, but he is also born with the whole animal heritage. Somehow we have to empty out the animal heritage and create a space for the treasure to come to the conscious and be shared because it is one of the qualities of the treasure: the more you share it, the more you have it.

Many of our problems are just there because we have never looked at them, never focused our eyes on them to figure out what they are.

Give life to things which are beautiful. Don't give life to ugly things. You don't have much time, much energy to waste. With such a small life, with such a small energy source, it is simply stupid to waste it in sadness, in anger, in hatred, in jealousy.

Use it in love, use it in some creative act, use it in friendship, use it in meditation: Do something with your energy which takes you higher. And the higher you go, the more energy sources become available to you. It is in your hands.

No man is an island. This has to be remembered as one of the fundamental truths of life. I am emphasizing it because we tend to forget it.

We are all part of one life force part of one, oceanic existence. Basically, because we are one deep down in our roots, the possibility of love arises. If we were not one, there would be no possibility of love.

Man still carries much of the animal instincts his anger, his hatred, his jealousy, his possessiveness, his cunningness. All that has been condemned in man seems to belong to a very deep-rooted unconscious. And the whole work of spiritual alchemy is how to get rid of the animal past.

Without getting rid of the animal past, man will remain divided. The animal past and his humanity cannot exist as one, because humanity has just the opposite qualities. So all that man can do is become a hypocrite.

As far as formal behavior is concerned, he follows the ideals of humanity of love and truth, freedom, non-possessiveness, compassion. But it remains only a very thin layer, and at any moment the hidden animal can come up; any accident can bring it up. And whether it comes up or not, the inner consciousness is divided.

This divided consciousness has been creating the yearning and the question: How to become a harmonious whole as far as the individual is concerned? And the same is true about the whole society: How can we make the society a harmonious whole where there is no war, no conflict, no classes; no divisions of color, caste, religion, nation?

Instead of thinking in terms of revolution and changing the society, its structure, we should think more of meditation and changing the individual. That is the only possible way that some day we can drop all divisions in the society. But first they have to be dropped in the individual – and they can be dropped.

There is not something labeled 'TRUTH' that one day you will find and open the box and see the contents and say, 'Great! I have found the truth!'

There is no such box.

The reason is clear why people talk about truth, and still remain in the world of lies. There is a longing in their heart for the truth; they are ashamed in front of themselves for their not being true, so they talk about truth. But it is mere talk. To live according to it is too dangerous, they cannot risk it.

And the same is the case with freedom. Everybody wants freedom as far as talking is concerned but nobody really is free. And nobody really wants to be free, because freedom brings responsibility; it does not come alone. And to be dependent is simple; the responsibility is not on you, the responsibility is on the person on whom you are dependent.

So people have make a schizophrenic way of life. They talk about truth, they talk about freedom and they live in lies and they live in slavery...slaveries of many kinds, because each slavery frees you from some responsibility. A man who really wants to be free has to accept immense responsibilities. He cannot dump his responsibilities on anybody else. Whatever he does, whatever he is, he is responsible.

A really non-violent person is one who does not kill anybody, does not harm anybody, because he is against killing and against harming. But if somebody starts harming him, then too, he is against harming. If somebody starts killing him, then too, he is against killing; he won't allow it.

He will never initiate any violence, but if violence is initiated against him, then he is going to fight tooth and nail. Only then can the non-violent people remain independent; otherwise they will be slaves, and poor, and continuously robbed.

To be yourself gives you all that you need to feel fulfilled, all that can make your life meaningful, significant. Just being yourself and growing according to your nature will bring the fulfillment of your destiny.

Be unpredictable and be ever-changing. Never stop changing and never stop being unpredictable; only then can life be a joy.
The moment you become predictable, you become a machine.

A machine is predictable. It was the same yesterday, it is the same today, it will be the same tomorrow. It is unchanging. It is only man's prerogative to be changing every moment.

The day you stop changing, in a subtle way you have died.

Put everything at stake. Be a gambler! Risk everything, because the next moment is not certain, so why bother? Why be concerned?

Live dangerously, live joyously. Live without fear, live without guilt. Live without any fear of hell, or any greed for heaven.

Just live.

Every error is an opportunity to learn. Just don't commit the same mistake again and again – that is stupidity. But commit as many new mistakes as you are capable of don't be afraid – because that is the only way nature allows you to learn.

Religiousness simply means a challenge to grow, a challenge for the seed to come to its ultimate peak of expression, to burst forth in thousands of flowers and release the fragrance that was hidden in it.

That fragrance I call religiousness.

Everybody is so miserable that he wants to find some reason somewhere to explain to himself why he is miserable, why she is miserable. And the society has given you a good strategy: Judge.

First, naturally you judge yourself about everything. No man is perfect, and no man can ever be perfect, perfection does not exist so judgment is very easy. You are imperfect, so there are things which show your imperfection. And then you are angry, angry with yourself, angry with the whole world: Why am I not perfect? And then you look with only one idea to find imperfection in everybody.

And then you want to open your heart and naturally because unless you open your heart, in your life there is no celebration, your life is almost dead. But you cannot do it directly. You will have to destroy all this upbringing from the very roots.

So the first thing is: Stop judging yourself.

Instead of judging, start accepting yourself with all the imperfections, all the frailties, all the mistakes, all the failures. Don't ask yourself to be perfect. That is simply asking for something impossible, and then you will feel frustrated.

You are a human being after all.

Just look at the animals, at the birds: nobody is worried, nobody is sad, nobody is frustrated. You don't see a buffalo freaking out. It is perfectly contented chewing the same grass every day. It is almost enlightened! There is no tension, there is tremendous harmony with nature, with itself, with everything as it is.

Buffaloes don't make parties to revolutionize the world, to change buffaloes into super-buffaloes, to make buffaloes religious, virtuous. No animal is concerned at all with human ideas.

And they must all be laughing: 'What has happened to you? Why can't you be just yourself as you are? What is the need to be somebody else?'

So the first thing is a deep acceptance of yourself.

Don't condemn sensuality. It has been condemned by the whole world, and because of their condemnation, the energy that can flower in sensuality moves into perversions, jealousy, anger, hatred a kind of life which is dry, with no juice.

Sensuousness is one of the greatest blessings to humanity. It is your sensitivity, it is your consciousness. It is your consciousness filtering through the body.

Parents have carried the idea down through the ages that children belong to them and have to be just carbon copies of them. A carbon copy is not a beautiful thing, and existence does not believe in carbon copies it rejoices in originality.

You have to help them to grow beyond you. You have to help them not to imitate you. That is really the duty of the parents to help the children not to fall into imitation. Children are imitative, and naturally, whom are they going to imitate? the parents are the closest people.

Up to now parents have enjoyed it very much, that their children are just like them. The father feels proud because his son is just like him. Then one life is wasted; then his son is not needed, he was enough.

Because of this wrong conception of pride in children imitating you, we have created a society of imitators.

Obedience needs no intelligence. All machines are obedient. Nobody has ever heard of a disobedient machine.

Obedience is simple too. It takes the burden off you of any responsibility. There is no need to react, you have simply to do what is being said. The responsibility rests with the source from where the order comes. In a certain way you are very free: you cannot be condemned for your act.

Religiousness is not something to be believed in, but something to be lived, something to be experienced...not a belief in your mind but the flavor of your whole being.

Mind cannot be non-judgmental. If you force it to be non-judgmental, there will arise a block in your intelligence. Then the mind cannot function perfectly. To be non-judgmental is not something which comes within the area of the mind. Only a man who has gone beyond mind can be non-judgmental; otherwise, what appears to you to be factual, a valid statement, is just an appearance.

Everything that mind decides or states is polluted by its conditioning, by its prejudices – that's what makes it judgmental.

For example, you see a thief. It is a fact that he has been stealing no question about it – and you make a statement about the thief. And certainly, stealing is not good; so when you call a man a thief, your mind says, 'You are valid; your statement is true.'

But why is a thief bad? and what is badness? Why has he been forced to steal? And the act of stealing is a single act: on the grounds of a single act you are making a judgment about the whole person. You are calling him a thief. He does many other things too, not only stealing.

He may be a good painter, he may be a good carpenter, he may be a good singer, a good dancer – there can be a thousand and one qualities in the man. The whole man is too big, and the stealing is a single action.

On the grounds of a single act, you cannot make a statement about the whole person. You don't know the person at all, and you don't even know the act, in what conditions it happened. Perhaps in those conditions you would have stolen too. Perhaps in those conditions stealing was not bad – because every act is relative to conditions.

If you look around the world and you see different people's conditionings, and their ideas of good and bad, right and wrong, you will for the first time be able to see that your mind is also part of a certain section of humanity. It does not represent anything about truth; it simply represents that certain section.

And through this mind, whatever you see is judgmental.

Existence is one. Its expressions are millions, but the spirit that is expressed is the same. It is one godliness with an infinite variety of creations.

Money is a strange thing. If you do not have it, it is a simple matter you don't have it there is no complexity. But if you have it, then it certainly creates complexities.

One of the greatest problems that money creates is, you never know whether you are desirable, or your money is desirable. And it is so difficult to figure it out that one would have preferred not to have money. At least life would have been simple.

Now, something like money that could have been a great pleasure has turned out to be immense anguish. But it is not the money, it is your mind.

Money is useful, there is no sin in having money, there is no need to feel guilt.

This is how mind creates misery. You have money, enjoy it. And if somebody loves you, do not pose this question, because you are putting the person in a really bad situation: If he says he loves you, you are not going to believe him, and if he says he loves your money, you are going to believe him. But if he loves your money, then the whole affair is finished. Deep down you will go on suspecting that he loves your money; it is not you.

But there is nothing wrong: the money is yours, just as your nose is yours, and your eyes are yours, and your hair is yours. And this man loves you in your totality. The money is also part of you. Don't separate it, then there is no problem.

Try to live a life with as little complexity and as few problems as possible and it is in your hands.

To know the whole world is nothing when it is compared to knowing your own inner mystery of life.

The very idea of comparison is absolutely false. Each individual is unique because there is nobody else like him. Comparison would have been right if all individuals were alike they are not. Even twins are not absolutely alike. It is impossible to find another man who is exactly like you. So we are comparing unique people, which creates the whole trouble.

One of the most difficult, but one of the most fundamental things of life is not to divide life into beautiful things and idiotic things, not to divide at all. They are all part of one whole.

It needs just a little sense of humor. And to me a sense of humor is very essential for a person to be whole.

What is wrong with small, idiotic things? Why can't you laugh and enjoy them? All the time you are judging what is right, what is wrong. All the time you are sitting in the seat of a judge – and that makes you serious.

Then flowers are beautiful, but what about the thorns? they are part of the existence of flowers. Flowers will not exist without the thorns; the thorns are protective. They have a function, a purpose, a meaning.

But when you divide then flowers are beautiful and thorns become ugly. But in the tree itself it is the same juice that goes into the flower and into the thorn. In the existence of the tree there is no division, no judgment. The flower in not favored, the thorn is not just tolerated; they are both accepted totally. And this should be our approach in our own life.

There are things, small things which, if you judge, look stupid, idiotic. But that is because of your judgment; otherwise they also fulfill something essential.

Mind's whole function is to go on dividing. The function of the heart is to see the joining link, about which the mind is completely blind.

The mind cannot understand that which is beyond words; it can understand only that which is linguistically, logically right. It has no concern with existence, with life, with reality. Mind itself is a fiction.

You can live without mind.

You cannot live without heart.

And the deeper you live, the more of your heart is involved.

Life is flowing, it is a river, a constant flux. People think of themselves as static. Only things are static, only death is unchanging life is constantly changing. More life and more change. Abundant life and there is tremendous change each moment.

Nobody is superior, nobody is inferior, and nobody is equal either. Everybody is unique. Equality is psychologically wrong. Everybody cannot be an Albert Einstein and everybody cannot be a Rabindranath Tagore. But that does not mean that Rabindranath Tagore is superior because you cannot be him. Rabindranath cannot be you either.

My whole point is that everybody is a unique manifestation. So we should destroy the whole idea of superiority and inferiority, equality and inequality, and replace it with a new concept of uniqueness.

And every individual is unique.

Just look lovingly and you will see that every individual has something which nobody else has.

Just do whatsoever is pleasant – pleasant to you and pleasant to your surroundings. Just do something which brings a song to you and creates a rhythm of celebration around you.

This life I call a religious life.

It has no principles, it has no discipline, it has no laws. It has only one, single approach – and that is, live intelligently.

Obedience has a simplicity; disobedience needs a little higher order of intelligence. Any idiot can be obedient in fact only idiots can be obedient.

The person of intelligence is bound to ask, 'Why? Why am I supposed to do this? And unless I know the reasons and the consequences of it, I am not going to be involved in it.' Then he is becoming responsible.

It is absolutely impossible for a saint to be a rascal but a rascal can be a saint.

Man has not learned yet to know the beauties of aloneness. He is always hankering for some relationship, to be with someone with a friend, with a father, with a wife, with a husband, with a child...with someone.

He has created societies, he has created clubs – the Lion's club, the Rotary club. He has created parties political, ideological. He has created religions, churches. But the basic need of all is to forget somehow that you are alone. Being associated with so many crowds, you are trying to forget something which in darkness suddenly is remembered that you were born alone, that you will die alone, that whatever you do, you live alone.

Aloneness is something so essential to your being, there is no way to avoid it.

Every effort that has been directed to avoid loneliness has failed, and will fail because it is against the fundamentals of life. What is needed is not something in which you can forget your loneliness; what is needed is that you become aware of your aloneness – which is a reality.

And it is so beautiful to experience it, to feel it, because it is your freedom from the crowd, from the other. It is our freedom from the fear of being lonely. Just the word 'lonely' immediately reminds you that it is like a wound: something is needed to fill it. It is a gap, and it hurts. Something needs to be filled into it.

Aloneness the very word does not have the same sense of a wound, of a gap, which has to be filled. Aloneness simply means completeness. You are whole; there is no need of anybody else to complete you.

So try to find out your innermost center where you are always alone, have always been alone. In life, in death wherever you are you will be alone. But it is so full it is not empty – it is so full and so complete and so overflowing with all the juices of life, with all the beauties and benedictions of existence, that once you have tasted your aloneness, the pain in the heart will disappear. Instead, a new rhythm of tremendous sweetness, peace, joy, bliss, will be there.

It does not mean that a man who is centered in his aloneness, complete in himself, cannot make friends in fact, only he can make friends because now it is no longer a need, it is just sharing. He has so much, he can share.

We are part of one existence. Whomsoever you are hurting, you are hurting yourself in the long run. Today you may not realize it, but one day when you become more aware; then you will say, 'My God! This wound was inflicted by me upon myself.' You had hurt somebody else thinking that people are different.

Nobody is different. This whole existence is one, cosmic unity. Out of this understanding comes non-violence.

When you are angry, you are punishing yourself. You are burning, you are destroying your heart and its higher qualities and you are full of hate.

Man is full if he is in tune with the universe. If he is not in tune with the universe then he is empty, utterly empty; and out of that emptiness comes greed.

Greed is to fill it with money, with houses, with furniture, with friends, with lovers, with anything because you cannot live as emptiness. It is horrifying. It is a ghost life. If you are empty and there is nothing inside you, it is impossible to live.

To have the feeling you have much inside you, there are only two ways. Either you get in tune with the universe...then you are filled with the whole, with all the flowers and with all the stars. That is real fulfillment.

But if you don't do that and millions of people are not doing that then there is just the way of filling yourself with any junk.

Greed simply means you are feeling a deep emptiness and you want to fill it with anything possible; it doesn't matter what it is.

Once you understand this, then you have nothing to do with greed. You have something to do with your coming into communion with the whole so the inner emptiness disappears.

The whole of the human past has been praising poverty and making it equal to spirituality, which is absolute nonsense.

Spirituality is the greatest richness that can happen to a man. It contains all other richnesses. It is not against any other richness, it is simply against all kinds of poverty.

On the one hand people will respect poverty, and on the other hand they will say, 'Serve the poor.' Strange! If poverty is so spiritual then the most spiritual thing will be to make every rich man, poor. Help the rich man to be poor, so he can become spiritual. Why help the poor? Do you want to destroy his spirituality?

To live in abundance is the only spiritual thing in the world.

Money is a loaded subject, for the simple reason that we have not been able to work out a sane system in which money can be a servant to the whole humanity, and not a master to a few greedy people.

Money is a loaded subject because man's psychology is full of greed. Otherwise, money is a simple means of exchanging things, a perfect means; there is nothing wrong in it. But the way we have worked it out, everything seems to be wrong in it.

If you don't have money, you are condemned, your whole life is a curse. And your whole life you are trying to have money by any means.

If you have money, it does not change the basic thing you want more, and there is no end to wanting more. And when finally you have so much money although it is not enough, it is never enough, but it is more than anybody else has then you start feeling guilty because the means you have used to accumulate the money are ugly, inhuman, violent. You have been exploiting, you have been sucking the blood of people, you have been a parasite. So now you have got the money, but it reminds you of all the crimes that you have committed in gaining it.

That creates two kinds of people: one, who starts donating to charitable institutions to get rid of guilt; and the other who feels so guilty that either he goes mad or commits suicide. His own existence becomes just anguish.

Each breath becomes heavy. And the strange thing is that he has worked his whole life to attain all this moey, because the society provokes the desire, the ambition, to be rich, to be powerful.

And money does bring power; it can purchase everything, except those few things which cannot be purchased by it. But nobody bothers about those things.

Meditation cannot be purchased, love cannot be purchased, friendship cannot be purchased, gratitude cannot be purchased but nobody is concerned with these things.

Just look at existence and its abundance. What is the need of so many flowers in the world? Just roses would have been enough. But existence is abundant millions and millions of flowers, millions of birds, millions of animals – everything in abundance.

Nature is not ascetic, it is dancing everywhere in the ocean, in the trees. It is singing everywhere in the wind passing through the pine trees, in the birds....

What is the need of millions of solar systems, of each solar system having millions of stars? There seems to be no need, except that abundance is the very nature of existence; that richness is the very core; that existence does not believe in poverty.

I don't see greed as a desire. It is some existential sickness. You are not in tune with the whole; and only that tuning with the whole can make you holy.

To me, greed is not a desire at all, so you need not do anything about greed. You have to understand that emptiness you are trying to fill and ask the question, 'Why am I empty? The whole existence is so full, why am I empty? Perhaps I have lost track. I am no longer moving in the same direction. I am no longer existential that is the cause of my emptiness.'

So be existential, let go, and move closer to existence in silence and peace, in meditation. And one day you will see you are so full, overfull, overflowing with joy, blissfulness, benediction. You have so much of it that you can give it to the whole world and yet it will not be exhausted.

That day, for the first time, you will not feel any greed for money, for food, for things – for anything. You will live, not with a greed that cannot be fulfilled, a wound that cannot be healed; you will live naturally, and whatever is needed, you will find it.

Everybody feels inferior in some way or other. And the reason is that we don't accept that everybody is unique. There is no question of inferiority or superiority. Everybody is just one of his kind comparison does not arise.

We have not allowed people to accept themselves as they are. The moment you accept yourself as you are, without any comparison, all inferiority, all superiority, disappears. In the total acceptance of yourself you will be free from these complexes inferiority, superiority. Otherwise you will suffer your whole life.

And I cannot conceive of a person who can have everything in this world. People have tried, and failed utterly.

Just be yourself, and that's enough.

You are accepted by the sun, you are accepted by the moon, you are accepted by the trees, you are accepted by the ocean, you are accepted by the earth. What more do you want?

You are accepted by this whole universe.

Rejoice in it!

To have approval and be recognized is everybody's need. Our whole life's structure is such that we are taught that unless there is recognition, we are nobody, we are worthless. Our work is not important, but the recognition. And this is putting things upside down.

Our work should be important a joy in itself. You should work, not to be recognized but because you enjoy being creative. You love the work for its own sake. You work if you love it.

Don't ask for recognition. If it comes, take it easily. If it does not come, do not think about it. Your fulfillment should be in the work itself.

And if everybody learns this simple art of loving his work, whatever it is, enjoying it without asking for any recognition we would have a more beautiful and celebrating world; otherwise the world has trapped you in a miserable pattern. What you are doing is not good because you love it, because you do it perfectly, but because the world recognizes it, rewards it, gives you gold medals, Nobel prizes.

They have taken away the whole intrinsic value of creativity, and destroyed millions of people because you cannot give millions of people Nobel prizes. And you have created the desire for recognition in everybody, so nobody can work peacefully, silently, enjoying whatever he is doing. And life consists of small things. For those small things there are not rewards, not titles given by the governments, not honorary degrees given by the universities.

Any man who has any sense of his individuality, lives by his own love, by his own work, without caring at all what others think of it.

The joy is not in completing something; the joy is that you desired it, that you desired it with your total intensity, that while you were doing it you had forgotten everything, the whole world; it was the only focus of your whole being.

And there is your bliss and your reward not in the completion, not in the permanence of anything.

In this changing flux of existence we have to find in each moment its own reward. Whatever we were doing, we did our best, we were not half-hearted. We were not keeping back something, but putting our total being into the act.

That's where our bliss is.

It is simply a fact that everybody is unique, and everybody has a certain individuality. We just have to drop ideas of how people should be, and we have to replace it with a philosophy that however people are, they are beautiful. There is no question of 'should be,' because who are we to impose any 'should' on anybody? If existence is to accept you as you are, then who am I not to?

So just a change of attitude and it is a very simple thing once it gets into your vision: Everybody is unique, everybody is as he is, and he should be as he is. There is no need for him to be somebody else to be accepted; he is accepted already. This is what I call respect for individuality, respect for people as they are.

The whole humanity can be such a loving and rejoicing place if we can accept people as they are.

A communism that comes out of love, out of intelligence, out of generosity, will be real. A communism that comes through force is going to be unreal.

And there is not a single man in the world, howsoever poor, who has nothing to contribute.

W hy not create a life where money does not create a hierarchy, but simply gives more and more opportunity to everybody?

T he people who are authoritarian are the people who are suffering from an inferiority complex.

To hide their inferiority they impose their superiority. They want to prove that they are somebody, that their word is truth, that their word is law. But deep down they are very inferior beings.

Nature certainly has no hierarchy. Hierarchy is man's mind game, because without a hierarchy the ego cannot feel nourished; it dies.

In nature, everything has an opportunity, space, and there is nobody being boss. Nobody is master and nobody is servant. Nature functions almost as an organic unity in which individuality is not lost, but in which the ego has no chance to evolve; hence trees don't have egos, birds don't have egos. Animals of all kinds don't have egos.

The problem arises with man.

It is man's privilege only man's privilege – to be alone, to stand against the whole world if he feels that he is with the truth.

If you feel that this is the way that leads to freedom, then accept any kind of responsibility. Then all those responsibilities are not going to be a burden on you. They are all going to make you more mature, more centered, more rooted, more of a beautiful individual.

You have only one moment in your hands the real moment. And you will not get this moment again. Either you live it or you leave it unlived.

Every child understands it, that he sees the world in a different way from his parents. As far as seeing is concerned, it is absolutely certain.

His values are different. He may collect seashells on the beach, and the parents will say, 'Throw them away. Why are you wasting your time?' And for him they were so beautiful.

He can see the difference, he can see that their values are different. The parents are running after money; he wants to collect butterflies. He can't see why they are so very interested in money: 'What are you going to do with it?' And his parents cannot see what he is going to do with these butterflies, or these flowers.

Every child comes to know this, that there are differences. The only problem is, he is afraid to assert that he is right.

As far as he is concerned, he should be left alone. It is a question of just a little courage – which is not missing in children either, it is just that the whole society is managed in such a way that even a beautiful quality like courage in a child will be condemned.

If parents really love children they will help them to be courageous even courageous against them. They will help them to be courageous against teachers, against society, against anybody who is going to destroy their individuality.

Remember never to compromise. Compromise is absolutely against my whole vision. You see people they are miserable because they have compromised on every point, and they cannot forgive themselves because they have compromised. They know that they could have dared, but they proved cowards. In their own eyes they have fallen, they have lost self-respect. That's what compromise does.

Why should one compromise? What have we got to lose? In this small life, live as totally as possible. Don't be afraid of going to the extreme. You cannot be more than total that is the last line. And don't compromise. Your whole mind will speak for compromise, because that's how we have been brought up, conditioned.

'Compromise' is one of the most ugly words in our language. It means, 'I give half, you give half; I settle for half, you settle for half.' But why? When you can have the whole, when you can eat the cake and have it too, then why compromise!

Just a little courage, just a little daring – and it is only in the beginning. Once you have experienced the beauty of non-compromising and the dignity that it brings, and the integrity and the individuality, for the first time you feel that you have roots, that you live out of a center that is your own.

The miserable person is easily enslaved. The cheerful person, the blissful person, cannot be enslaved.

Sex is the beginning of life, and death is the end of the same life; so they are the two ends of one energy, two poles of one energy. They cannot be unconnected.

Perhaps sex is death in installments.

And death is sex wholesale.

But there is certainly one energy functioning at both corners.

Why not create a life where sex does not make bitter experiences, jealousies, failures; where sex becomes just fun nothing more than any other game, just a biological game.

You play tennis; that does not mean your whole life you have to play tennis with the same partner.

Life should be richer. It is only that a little understanding is needed, and love will not be a problem, sex will not be taboo.

Mind is simply a collection of memories of the past, and out of those memories – imaginations about the future.

Use every opportunity in life for raising your intelligence, your consciousness. Ordinarily what we are doing is that we are using every opportunity to make a hell for ourselves. Only you suffer, and because of your suffering, you make others suffer.

And when so many people are living together, if they all create suffering for each other, it goes on multiplying. That's how the whole world has become a hell.

It can be instantly changed, just the basic thing has to be understood: Without intelligence there is no heaven.

According to me, the function of the parents is not to help the children to grow; they will grow without you.

Your function is to support, to nourish, to help what is already growing. Don't give directions and don't give ideals. Don't tell them what is right and what is wrong let them find it by their own experience.

The whole idea that children are your possession is wrong. They are born through you, but they do not belong to you. You have a past, they have only a future.

They are not going to live according to you. To live according to you will be almost equivalent to not living at all. They have to live according to themselves in freedom, in responsibility, in danger, in challenge.

Once you understand that your children do not belong to you, that they belong to existence and you have been just a passage, you have to be grateful to existence that it has chosen you to be a passage for a few beautiful children. But you are not to interfere in their growth, in their potential. You are not to impose yourself upon them.

They are not going to live in the same times, they are not going to face the same problems. They will be part of another world. Don't prepare them for this world, this society, this time, because then you will be creating troubles for them. They will find themselves unfit, unqualified.

Cruelty is a misunderstanding. It arises in us because of the fear of death. We don't want to die, so before anybody else kills you, you would like to kill him because the best method of defense is attack. And you don't know who is going to attack you.

In the animal kingdom, in the human world, there is a tremendous competition, so people simply go on attacking, not bothering whom they are attacking, or whether he was really going to attack them. But there is no way to find out it is better not to take a chance.

And when you attack somebody, slowly slowly your heart becomes harder and harder, and you start enjoying attacking. The phenomenon can be seen in the animals because the same competition for food, for power....

Cruelty is nothing but a competitive spirit to be the first. If it means violence, then violence; but one has to be the first. It is there in the animals, it is in man. But why this rush to be the first?

The existential reason is death.

Cruelty disappears only and that's how I find the clue as to why cruelty is only when you know there is no death. When you experience something immortal in you, all cruelty disappears. Then it does not matter; you need not run, you can let the other go ahead of you because the poor fellow does not know that the world is infinite, life is infinite.

There is no way of missing anything; if it does not happen today, then tomorrow. But you cannot miss anything if you understand.

In fact, in fighting and being cruel to each other, and violent, you may miss much because this whole process will harden you, will make a stone of your heart. And the heart, if turned into a stone, is going to miss all that is great, all that is beautiful, all that is blissful.

It is difficult to explain to the animals. But the real problem is, it is even difficult to explain to human beings that through competition, violent ambition, reaching everywhere first, you are creating an insane world in which nobody enjoys anything, and everybody remains poor.

The only way to make people understand is to help them to feel their immortal self, and immediately all cruelty will disappear. It is the shortness of life that is making the trouble. If you have infinity on both ends past and future – there is no need to be in a hurry, no need to compete even. Life is so much and so full, you cannot exhaust it.

Those who want just to think about life, about living, about love for them, past and future are perfectly beautiful because they give them infinite scope. They can decorate their past, make it as beautiful as they like although they never lived it; when it was present they were not there. These are just shadows, reflections. They were continuously running, and while running they have seen a few things they think they have lived.

In the past, only death is the reality, not life.

In the future also, only death is the reality, not life.

Those who have missed living, in the past, to substitute for the gap automatically start dreaming about the future. Their future is only a projection out of the past. Whatever they have missed in the past, they are hoping for in the future; and between these two non-existences is the small existent moment, which is life.

Time is thought to consist of three tenses – past, present, future which is wrong. Time consists only of past and future.

It is life which consists of the present.

So those who want to live, for them there is no other way than to live this moment.

Only the present is existential.

Past is simply a collection of memories, and future is nothing but your imagination, your dreams.

Reality is here now.

The present has nothing to do with time. If you are just here in this moment, there is no time. There is immense silence, stillness, no movement; nothing is passing, everything has come to a sudden stop.

The present gives you the opportunity to dive deep into the water of life, or to fly high into the sky of life.

But on both sides there are dangers 'past' and 'future' are the most dangerous words in human language. Between past and future, living in the present is almost like walking on a tightrope; on both sides there is danger.

But once you have tasted the juices of the present, you don't care about dangers. Once you are in tune with life then nothing matters.

And to me, life is all there is.

For those who want to live not to think about it, but to love; not to think about it; but to be; not to philosophize about it there is no other alternative: then drink the present moment's juices. Squeeze it totally because it is not going to come back again. Once gone, it is gone forever.

Life is spread over seventy, eighty years; death happens in a single moment. It is so condensed that if you have lived your life rightly, you will be able to enter into the mystery of death. And the mystery of death is that it is only a cover: inside is your immortality, your eternal life.

I don't think much about the future because the future is born of the present. If we can take care of the present, we have taken care of the future.

The future is not going to come from nowhere, it going to grow from this moment. The next moment will be growing out of this moment.

If this moment is beautiful, silent, blissful, the next moment is bound to be more silent, more blissful.

To me, seriousness is a sickness; and a sense of humor makes you more human, more humble. A sense of humor according to me is one of the most essential parts of religiousness.

Man need not transcend nature. I say unto you, man has to fulfill nature which no animal can do. That is the difference.

You are born as a natural being. You cannot go above yourself. It is like pulling yourself up by pulling on your legs. You may hop a little, but sooner or later you are going to fall on the ground and may have a few fractures. You cannot fly.

And that's what has been done: People have been trying to raise themselves above nature, which means above themselves. But they are not separate from nature.

Man has the capacity, the intelligence, the freedom, to explore and if you have explored nature totally, you have come home.

Nature is your home.

It is one of the fundamental laws of life that everything that is higher is very vulnerable. The roots of a tree are very strong, but not the flowers. The flowers are very vulnerable just a strong breeze and the flower may be destroyed.

The same is true about human consciousness. Hate is very strong, but not love. Love is just like a flower easily crushed by any stone, destroyed by any animal.

The higher values of life have to be protected.

The lower values have a certain protection of themselves.

A stone need not be protected, but just by the side of it the rose in the bush has to be protected. The stone is dead, it cannot become more dead. It does not need protection.

But the rose is so alive, so beautiful, so colorful, so attractive. That is the danger it is its strength, but it is inviting danger. Somebody may pluck it. Nobody will take up the stone, but the flower can be plucked.

Love should be made at the highest peak and that needs a certain discipline. People have used discipline not to make love. I teach discipline to make love rightly, so that your love is not just a biological thing that never reaches to your psychological world.

Love has the potential to reach even to your spiritual world, and at the highest peak it will reach to your spiritual world.

Orgasm is not something necessary for reproduction. It is something to open a window for the higher evolution of consciousness.

The experience of orgasm is always non-sexual. Even if you have achieved it through sex, it itself has no sexuality in it.

That gives the insight that there may be possibilities of reaching it through non-sexual means, because it is non-sexual itself, so sexuality is not necessarily the only way.

Whoever first experienced this must have concluded that there can be other ways to reach orgasm because sex is not necessarily a part in it. It does not leave any color, any impression of sex in it.

Then he must have watched how it happens, and then things are very clear: the moment the orgasm happens, time stops, you forget about time. Your mind stops, you do not think anymore. There is tremendous calmness, and a great awareness.

Any observer going through the experience will naturally think, 'If these things can be managed without sex awareness, thoughtlessness, timelessness you will reach to the orgasmic state, by-passing sexuality.' And this is my understanding: this is how man must have first discovered meditation.

Freedom simply makes you absolutely responsible for everything that you are and that you are going to be.

There are people who become angry: these are the people who create revolutions, changes in the society, in the state. But all their revolutions have failed, because anything coming out of anger is coming out of ignorance. It is not going to create an authentic change.

Change for the better is impossible out of anger. I want you to remember one thing that sadness is just anger upside down. It is not different; it is repressed anger. If you analyze it then you will see the fact. Sadness can change into anger very easily; anger can change into sadness in the same way. They are not two things...perhaps two sides of the same coin.

The world is sad, it is in misery. There is a great suffering in the hearts of people. But you need not be sad about it, for the simple reason that by becoming sad you join them; you create more sadness. It is not a help.

It is just as if people are sick, and you see their sickness and you also become sick. Your sickness is not going to make them healthy; it is simply creating more sickness. To feel for their sickness means to look for the causes, at what is creating all their suffering and misery, and to help them to remove those causes.

And at the same time you have to remain as joyful as possible because your joy is going to help them not your sadness. You have to be cheerful. They should know that there is a possibility of being cheerful in this sad world....

Anger is always
a sign of weakness.

Times of disaster make you aware of the reality as it is. It is always fragile, everybody is always in danger. It is just that in ordinary times you are fast asleep, so you don't see it. You go on dreaming, imagining beautiful things for the coming days, for the future.

And in moments when danger is imminent, then suddenly you become aware that there may be no future, no tomorrow, that this is the only moment you have got.

The times of disaster are very revealing. They don't bring anything new in the world; they simply make you aware of the world as it is. They wake you up. If you don't understand this, you can go mad; if you understand this, you can become awakened.

It is pointless to be worried, because you will be only missing this moment, and you won't help anybody. So that's the secret of how to transcend the danger.

The secret is: Start living more fully, more totally, with more alertness, so that you can find within yourself something that is untouchable by death.

That is the only shelter, the only security, the only safety.

So it is only a question of how to use everything. Whatever it is, use it rightly.

The disaster is great, the danger is great, but great is the opportunity too.

No illusion can stand against reality. Reality is going to crush it sooner or later.

The function of a father or a mother is great, because they are bringing a new guest into the world who knows nothing, but who brings some potential in him. Unless his potential grows he will remain unhappy; and no parents can think of their children remaining unhappy.

They want them to be happy it is just that their thinking is wrong. They think if their children become doctors, if they become professors, engineers, scientists, then they will be happy. They don't know.

Their children can only be happy if they become what they have come to become. They can only become the seed that they are carrying within themselves.

Judgment is ugly, it hurts people. On the one hand you go on hurting them, wounding them, and on the other hand you want their love, their respect. It is impossible.

Love them, respect them, and perhaps your love and respect may help them to change many of their weaknesses, many of their failures because love will give them new energy, a new meaning, a new strength.

Love will give them new roots to stand against strong wind, hot sun, heavy rains.

Whenever there is a question of choice, the head cannot be chosen against the heart. The heart is your relationship with existence, and the head is your relationship with the society.

If you are sad you are wrong; if you are joyful you are right.

When I say, be cheerful, be happy, rejoice in the fact that you are not in the position of being miserable and suffering, I have a certain purpose behind it.

The purpose is that you have to become an example to those people who have completely forgotten that life can also be a rejoicing. In spite of all darkness you can still be unburdened by the darkness, you can still dance. Darkness cannot prevent your dance; it has no preventative force.

To me, this is real service.

The mind should be trained to be a servant of the heart. Logic should serve love.

And then life can become a festival of lights.

The ancient saying, 'As above, so below,' or vice-versa, contains one of the most foundational truths about mysticism. It means that there is no above, no below, that existence is one.

Divisions are created by the mind.

Existence is divisionless.

Divisions are our projections, and we get so identified with divisions that we lose contact with the whole.

Our mind is just a small window opening towards the vast universe, but when you look always from the window, the frame of the window frames the sky outside. Although there is no frame on the sky it is frameless to your perception the window frame becomes the frame of existence.

It is something like, once in a while people who use glasses it happens to them that they have their glasses on their nose and they are looking for them. They have even forgotten that they cannot see without the glasses, so if they are looking and seeing, it is an absolute certainty that the glasses are in place.

But if you have been using glasses for years, slowly slowly they become part of you; they become your eyes. You don't think of them as separate from you. But each pair of glasses can give its own color to the things it sees. You are the seer behind the glasses cannot see by themselves. Things outside don't have the color that the glass is imposing upon them, but you have become so identified with the glasses....

Man's mind is also only an instrument. The glasses are outside the skull, the mind is inside the skull so you cannot take it off every day. And you are so close to it within, that the very closeness has become the identification.

So whatever the mind sees is thought to be the reality. And mind cannot see the reality; mind can see only its own prejudices. It can see its own projections displayed on the screen of the world.

Against truth, the greatest enemy in the world is the knowledgeable person and the greatest friend is one who knows that he does not know.

We have been told, taught, programmed in such a way that even a thing like love has to be a mind thing.

Love is basically of the heart, but our whole society has tried to bypass the heart, because the heart is not logical, is not rational, and our mind has been trained through education that anything illogical is wrong, anything irrational is wrong: only a logical thing is right.

And in our educational programming there is no place for the heart; it is just of the mind. The heart has almost been removed from our existence, silenced. It has never been given a chance to grow, to have its potential become actual. So mind is dominating.

Mind is good when money is concerned, mind is good when war is concerned, mind is good when ambitions are concerned, but mind is absolutely useless when love is concerned. Money, war, desire, ambitions you cannot put love in the same category.

Love has a separate source in your being where there is no contradiction.

An authentic education will not only teach your mind because mind can give you a good livelihood, but not a good life. The heart cannot give you a good livelihood, but it can give you a good life. And there is no reason to choose between the two: use the mind for that which it is made, and use the heart for that which it is made.

Religions, politicians, business people, warriors all want the mind to be trained. And heart can be a disturbance, it is going to be a disturbance.

If you are a soldier and if you have a heart, you cannot kill the enemy. The moment you take your gun to kill someone, your heart will say, 'Just as you have a wife waiting for you – your children, your old mother and father this poor man's wife must be waiting also, his children, his old mother and father, waiting for the son to return home.'

He has not done anything to you, and you are going to kill him. For what? to get an award from the military academy? To get promotion?

If you think of society as becoming an ideal society, a paradise, it seems to be impossible: There are so many conflicts, and there seems to be no way to harmonize them.

A harmonious human society is possible, should be possible, because it will be the best opportunity for everyone to grow, the best opportunity for everyone to be himself. The richest possibilities will be available to everyone.

So it seems the way it is, society is absolutely stupid.

The utopians are not dreamers, but your so-called realists who condemn the utopians are stupid. But both are agreed on one point that something has to be done in the society.

They are all concerned with the society – and that is where their failure lies.

As I see it, utopia is not something that is not going to happen it is something that is possible, but we should go to the causes, not to the symptoms.

And the causes are in the individuals, not in the society.

Man has forgotten who he truly is. He has almost become auto-hypnotized with a certain idea about himself, and he carries that idea his whole life, without knowing that it is not he but only his shadow. And you cannot fulfill your shadow.

There is no need of any war, no need of any fight, no need of jealousy, no need of hate. Life is so short and love is so precious. And when you can fill your life with love, with harmony, with joy, when you can make your life a poetry unto itself if you miss, only you are responsible for it, nobody else.

It is only a question of understanding; a simple insight is needed not to be dragged down by the forces of darkness, negativity, destructiveness.

Just a little alertness is needed to devote yourself to creativity, to love, to sensitivity, and to make this small life just a series of songs – so that you dance in your life and your death will be the crescendo of your dance; so that you live totally and you die totally, with no complaint, but with gratitude, with thankfulness to existence.

Everybody wants to be loved. That is a wrong beginning. And it starts because the child, the small child, cannot love, cannot say anything, cannot do anything, cannot give anything he can only get.

A small child's experience of love is of getting getting from the mother, getting from the father, getting from the brothers, sisters, getting from guests, strangers, but always getting. So the first experience, deep in his unconscious settles that he has to get love.

But the trouble arises because everybody has been a child, and everybody has the same urge to get love; and nobody is born in any other way. So all are asking, 'Give us love,' and there is nobody to give, because the other person is also brought up in the same way.

So one has to be alert and aware that just an accident of birth should not remain a constant prevailing state of your mind. Rather than asking, 'Give me love,' start giving love. Forget about getting, simply give; and I guarantee you, you will get much.

Evolution functions through polarities. Just as you cannot walk on one leg, you need two legs to walk, existence needs polar opposites man and woman, life and death, love and hate to create momentum; otherwise there will be silence.

The opposite attracts you on the one hand, and on the other hand makes you feel dependent. And nobody wants to be dependent; hence there is a constant struggle between lovers. They are trying to dominate each other.

The name is love, but the game is politics.

The very effort of man is to dominate the woman, to reduce her to an inferior status, not allow her to grow so she always remains retarded.

The freedom of woman from man's slavery will also be a freedom for man to experience.

So I say the women's liberation movement is not only woman's liberation, it is also man's liberation movement; both will be liberated.

The slavery is binding them both, and there is continuous struggle. The woman has found her own strategies to harass the husband, to nag him, to put him down; and the man has his own strategy. And between these two fighting camps we have been hoping love is happening. Centuries have passed – love has not happened, or only once in a while.

This is the situation of the ordinary love, which is only love in name, not a reality.

If you ask my vision of love...it is no longer a question of dialectics, opposition. Man and woman are different and complementary. Man alone is half, so is woman. Only together, in a deep feeling of oneness, do they feel for the first time totality, perfection.

For thousands of years what man has done to woman is simply monstrous. She cannot think of herself as equal to man. And she has been conditioned so deeply that even if you say she is equal, she is not going to believe it. It has become almost her mind, the conditioning has become her mind, that she is less in everything physical strength, intellectual qualities.

And the man who has reduced the woman to such a state also cannot love her. Love can exist only in equality, in friendship.

If you can love without jealousy, if you can love without attachment, if you can love a person so much that his happiness is your happiness – even if he is with some other woman and he is happy, it makes you happy because you love him so much: his happiness is your happiness. You will be happy because he is happy, and you will be grateful to the woman who made the person you love happy you will not be jealous. Then love has come to a purity.

This love cannot create any bondage. And this love is simply the opening of the heart to all the winds, to the whole sky.

Jealousy is very complicated. It has many ingredients in it. Cowardice is one of them; egoistic attitudes is another; monopolistic desire – not an experience of love but only of possessiveness; a tendency to be competitive; a deep-rooted fear of being inferior.

So many things are involved in jealousy.

Risks should be one of the basic foundations of a real man. The moment you see that things are settling, unsettle them.

You are a crowd, a multitude. You just have to look more closely, more deeply, and you will find many people within you. And they all pretend at times to be you. When you are angry, a certain personality possesses you and pretends that this is you. When you are loving, then another personality possesses you and pretends this is you.

It is not only confusing to you, it is confusing to everybody who comes in contact with you, because they cannot figure it out. They themselves are a crowd.

And in each relationship there are not two persons getting married but two crowds getting married. There is going to be a great war continuously, because rarely will it be just by accident that your loving person is in charge and the other's loving person is in charge. Otherwise, you go on missing. You are loving, but the other is sad or angry or worried. And when he is in a loving state, you are not. And there is no way to bring on these personalities; they move of their own accord.

There is a certain rotation inside you, and if you go on watching don't interfere with these personalities because that will create more mess, more confusion. Just watch, because watching all these personalities you are going to become aware that there is a watcher too, which is not a personality, before whom these personalities come and go.

And it is not another personality, because one personality cannot watch another personality. This is something very interesting and very basic – that one personality cannot watch another personality, because those personalities don't have any soul.

It is like your clothes. You can go on changing your clothes, but your clothes cannot know that they have been changed, that now another piece of clothing is being used. You are not clothes, so you can change them. You are not a personality that's why you can become aware of these innumerable personalities.

But this also makes one point very clear, that there is something which goes on watching this whole game of personalities around you.

And this is you.

So watch these personalities, but remember that your watchfulness is your reality. And if you can remain watchful of the personality, those personalities will start disappearing; they cannot live. They need identification to remain alive. If you are angry it needs you to forget to watch and become identified with anger then anger has no life; it is already dead, dying, disappearing.

So remain more and more concentrated in your watchfulness, and all these personalities will disappear. And when there is no personality left, then your reality the master has come home.

Then you behave sincerely, authentically. Then whatever you do, you do totally, fully you never repent. You are always in a rejoicing mood.

Many of our problems perhaps most of our problems are because we have never looked at them face to face, encountered them; and not looking at them is giving them energy. Being afraid of them is giving them energy, always trying to avoid them is giving them energy – because you are accepting them. Your very acceptance is their existence. Other than your acceptance, they don't exist.

You have the source of energy. Whatever happens in your life needs your energy. If you cut the source of energy and in other words that's what I call identification if you don't identify with anything, it immediately becomes dead, it has no energy of its own.

And non-identification is the other side of watchfulness.

Habit is easy, consciousness is difficult – but only in the beginning.

We have never bothered about the roots of love, and we have talked only about the flowers. We say to people to be non-violent, to be compassionate, to be loving so much that you can love your enemy, so much that you can even love your neighbor.

We talk about flowers, but nobody is interested in the roots.

The question is, why are we not loving beings? It is not a question of being loving to this person, to that person, to the friend, to the enemy; the question is whether you are loving or not.

Do you love your own body? Have you ever cared to touch your own body with a loving caress? Do you love yourself?

You are wrong, and you have to put yourself right. You are a sinner, and you have to become a saint. How can you love yourself? You cannot even accept yourself. And these are the roots!

The plastic flowers are permanent the plastic love will be permanent. The real flower is not permanent; it is changing moment to moment. Today it is there, dancing in the wind and in the sun and in the rain. Tomorrow you will not be able to find it. It has disappeared just as mysteriously as it appeared.

Real love is like a real flower.

The heart knows nothing of the past, nothing of the future; it knows only of the present. The heart has no time concept.

Understand that past and future are both non-existential. All that you have got is a very small moment: this very moment. You don't even get another moment. You always have only one moment in your hands; and it is so small and so fleeting that if you are thinking of the past and the future, you will miss it. And that is the only life and the only reality there is.

Politics is a disease, and it should be treated exactly like that. And it is more dangerous than cancer: if surgery is needed, it should be done. But politics is basically dirty. And it has to be, because for one post thousands of people are hankering, longing. Then naturally they will fight, they will kill; they will do anything.

The whole program of our mind is so wrong in that we have been programmed to be ambitious and that's where politics is. It is not only in the ordinary world of politics, it has even polluted your ordinary life.

Even a small child starts smiling at the mother, at the father, with a bogus smile. There is no depth behind it, but he knows that whenever he smiles, he is rewarded. He has learned the first rule of being a politician. He is still in the cradle, and you have taught him politics. And then in human relationships everywhere, there is politics.

Man has crippled woman. It is politics. Woman constitutes half of humanity, and man has no right to completely cripple her; but for centuries he has been crippling her.

He has not allowed her education, he has not allowed her even to listen to the holy scriptures. In many religions he has not allowed her to to enter the temple; or, if he has allowed her, she has a separate section. She cannot stand with the man as equal even before God.

Man has tried to cut the freedom of woman in every way. This is politics; it is not love. You love a woman but you don't give her freedom. What kind of love is this, which is afraid of giving freedom? You encage her like a parrot. You can say you love the parrot, but you don't understand: you are killing the parrot.

You have taken away from the parrot his whole sky, and you have given him just a cage. The cage may be made of gold, but even a golden cage is nothing to be compared with the freedom of the parrots in the sky, moving from tree to tree, singing their song not what you force them to sing, but what is natural to them, what is authentic to them.

Half of humanity in every country, in every civilization, has been destroyed by family politics, but it is politics. Wherever there is the urge to have power over another person, it is politics.

Power is always political, even over small children. The parents think they love, but it is only in their mind; otherwise they want the children to be obedient. And what does obedience mean? It means all the power is in the hands of the parents.

If obedience is such a great quality, why shouldn't the parents be obedient to the children? If it is such a religious thing, parents should be obedient to children.

Power has nothing to do with religion. All that power has to do with religion is to hide politics in a beautiful word.

Man needs exposure on every point wherever politics has entered and it has entered everywhere, in every relationship. It has contaminated the whole of life and it is continuously contaminating it.

The ambition that is created is that you have to become someone in the world, that you have to prove that you are not an ordinary person, you are extraordinary. But for what? What purpose does it serve? It serves only one purpose: you become powerful, others become subservient to you.

You have castrated the whole of humanity in different ways and this castration is very political.

People love freedom but nobody wants responsibility. And they come together, they are inseparable.

Why should you bother about recognition? Bothering about recognition has meaning only if you don't love your work; then it is meaningful, then it seems to be a substitute. You hate the work, you don't like it, but you are doing it because there will be recognition; you will be appreciated, accepted.

Rather than thinking about recognition, reconsider your work.

Do you love it? Then that is the end. If you do not love it, then change it.

The parents, the teachers, are always insisting that you should be recognized, you should be accepted. This is a very cunning strategy to keep people in control.

Learn one basic thing. Do whatever you want to do, love to do, and never ask for recognition. That is begging. Why should one ask for recognition? Why should one hanker for acceptance?

Deep down in yourself, look. Perhaps you don't like what you are doing. Perhaps you are afraid that you are on the wrong track. Acceptance will help you feel that you are right. Recognition will make you feel that you are going towards the right goal.

The question is of your own inner feelings; it has nothing to do with the outside world. Why depend on others? and all these things depend on others; you yourself are becoming dependent.

When you avoid this dependence you become an individual and to be an individual, living in total freedom upon your own feet, drinking from your own sources, is what makes a man really centered, rooted. And that is the beginning of his ultimate flowering.

If intelligence remains innocent it is the most beautiful thing possible. But if intelligence is against innocence then it is simply cunningness and nothing else; it is not intelligence.

The moment innocence disappears, the soul of intelligence is gone, it is a corpse. It is better to call it simply 'intellect.' It can make you a great intellectual, but it will not transform your life and it will not make you open to the mysteries of existence.

These mysteries are open only to the intelligent child. And the really intelligent person keeps his childhood alive to his last breath. He never loses it the wonder the child feels looking at the birds, looking at the flowers, looking at the sky.... Intelligence also has to be, in the same way, childlike.

It is a strange thing that truth is not democratic. It is not to be decided by votes what is true; otherwise, we could never come to any truth ever. People will vote for what is comfortable and lies are very comfortable because you don't have to do anything about them, you have just to believe.

Truth needs great effort, discovery, risk, and it needs you to walk alone on a path which nobody has traveled before.

The qualities of a mature person are very strange. First, he is not a person, he is no longer a self.

He has a presence, but he is not a person.

Second: he is more like a child simple and innocent. That's why I said the qualities of a mature person are very strange, because 'maturity' gives the sense as if he is experienced, he is aged, old.

Physically he may be old, but spiritually he is an innocent child. His maturity is not just experience gained through life then he would not be a child, and then he would not be a presence. He would be an experienced person knowledgeable but not mature.

Maturity has nothing to do with your life experiences. It has something to do with your inward journey, experiences of the inner.

The more a person goes deeper into himself, the more mature he is. When he has reached to the very center of his being, he is perfectly mature. But at that moment the person disappears, only a presence remains; the self disappears, only silence remains. The knowledge disappears, only innocence remains.

To me, maturity is another name of realization. You have come to the fulfillment of your potential. It has become actual. The seed has come on the long journey and has blossomed.

Maturity has a fragrance. It gives a tremendous beauty to the individual. It gives intelligence, the sharpest possible intelligence. It makes him nothing but love. His action is love, his inaction is love. His life is love, his death is love. He is just a flower of love.

Every time one realizes something of the truth, there is a dance in the heart. The heart is the only testimony for the truth.

And it cannot testify through words. It can testify in its own way: through love, through dance, through playing music non-verbal. It speaks, but it does not speak in language and logic.

Modern music has fallen from grace because it has forgotten its basic purpose. It has forgotten its origin. It does not know that it has anything to do with meditation. And the same is true about other arts. They have all become non-meditative, and they are all leading people to madness.

The artist is creating a danger for himself and is also creating a danger for those who will be his audience. He may be a painter, but his painting is crazy; it has not come out of meditativeness.

Mind's whole function is to go on dividing. The function of the heart is to see the joining link about which the mind is completely blind.

Mediocre minds cannot go mad.

The thought of stillness and silence excites nobody. It is not your personal problem; it is the problem of the human mind as such, because to be still, to be silent, means to be in a state of no-mind.

Mind cannot be still. It needs continuous thinking, worrying. The mind functions like a bicycle: if you go on pedaling it, it continues; the moment you stop the pedaling, you are going to fall down. Mind is a two-wheel vehicle, just like a bicycle; and your thinking is a constant pedaling.

Even sometimes if you are a little bit silent, you immediately start worrying, 'Why am I silent?' Anything will do to create worrying, thinking, because mind can exist only in one way – in running, always running after something or running from something, but always running. In the running is the mind.

The moment you stop, the mind disappears.

We try in every way to drop the feeling of being strangers. That's why we have created all kinds of rituals. One man gets married to a woman; and what is marriage? just a ritual. But why? – because they want to drop that strangeness and somehow create a bridge.

The bridge is never created; they only imagine that now one is a husband, the other is a wife, but they remain strangers. Their whole life they will live together, but they will not be anything other than strangers, because nobody can penetrate into the other's aloneness.

You can only not be a stranger if you can penetrate into my aloneness, or I can penetrate into your aloneness which is not possible, not existentially possible. We can come as close as possible; but the closer we become, the more we will become aware of the strangeness, because the better we will be able to see, 'The other is unknown to me, and perhaps unknowable.'

Everybody has a kind of armor. There are reasons for it. First, the child is born so utterly helpless into a world he knows nothing of. Naturally he is afraid of the unknown that faces him.

He has not forgotten yet those nine months of absolute security, safety there was no problem, no responsibility, no worry for tomorrow. To us, those are nine months, but to the child it is eternity. He knows nothing of the calendar; he knows nothing of minutes, hours, days, months. He has lived an eternity in absolute safety and security, without any responsibility.

And then suddenly he is thrown into a world unknown, where he is dependent on everything, on others. It is natural that he will feel afraid. Everybody is bigger and powerful, and he cannot live without the help of others. He knows he is dependent; he has lost his independence, his freedom.

At one point the armor may be a necessity; perhaps it is. But as you grow, if you are not only growing old but also growing up growing in maturity then you will start seeing what you are carrying with you.

Look closely and you will find fear behind it. Anything that is connected with fear, a mature person should disconnect himself from. That's how maturity comes. Just watch all your acts, all your beliefs, and find out whether they are based in reality, in experience, or based in fear. And anything based in fear has to be dropped immediately without a second thought. It is your armor.

Your psychological armor cannot be taken away from you; you will fight for it. Only you can do something to drop it; and that is, to look at each and every part of it. If it is based in fear, then drop it. If it is based in reason, in experience, in understanding, then it is not something to be dropped but something to be made part of your being.

But you will not find a single thing in your armor which is based on experience. It is all fear, from A to Z. And we go on living out of fear; that's why we go on poisoning every other experience. We love somebody, but out of fear. It spoils, it poisons. We seek truth, but if it is out fear then you are not going to find it.

Whatever you do, remember one thing: out of fear you are not going to grow; you will only shrink and die. Fear is in the service of death.

A fearless person has everything that life wants to give to you as a gift. Now there is no barrier: you will be showered with gifts, and whatever you will be doing, you will have a strength, a power, a certainty, a tremendous feeling of authority.

What you have to understand is the process of identification, how one can get identified with something which one is not. Right now you are identified with the mind. You think you are it. From there comes the fear. If you are identified with the mind, then naturally, if the mind stops you are finished, you are no more. And you don't know anything beyond mind.

The reality is that you are not mind, you are something beyond mind; hence, it is absolutely necessary that the mind stops so that for the first time you can know that you are not mind because you are still there.

Mind is gone, you are still there; and with greater joy, greater glory, greater light greater consciousness, greater being.

The reality is that we are alone, we are strangers and the world will be far better if we accept it, a basic truth, that we are strangers.

And what is wrong with falling in love with a stranger? What is the need that before you fall in love with a stranger, the strangeness should be destroyed?

It is one of the beauties of life that we are all strangers, and there is no way to change this reality. It is beautiful to have strangers love you, to have strangers as your friends, to have strangers all around the world. Then the whole world becomes a mystery and it is a mystery.

Love allows freedom. Love allows that whatever the other feels like doing, he can do. Whatever he feels if it makes him blissful, it is his choice.

If you love the person, then you don't interfere in his privacy. You leave that person's privacy uninterfered with. You don't try to trespass his inner being.

Love's basic requirement is that, 'I accept the other person as he is.' And love never tries to change the person according to one's own idea of them. You do not try to cut the person here and there and bring him to size which is being done everywhere all over the world....

If you love, then there are no conditions to be put.

If you don't love, then who are you to put conditions?

Either way it is clear. If you love, then there is no question of conditions. You love him as he is. If you don't love, then too there is no problem. He is nobody to you; there is no question of putting conditions. He can do whatsoever he wants to do.

If jealousy disappears and still love remains, then you have something solid in your life which is worth having.

It is a known fact: you fall in love with a man; you don't fall in love with a real man, you fall in love with a man of your imagination. While you are not together, and you see the man from your balcony, or you meet the man on the seabeach for a few minutes, or you hold hands in a movie, you start feeling, 'We are made for each other.'

But nobody is made for each other. You go on projecting more and more imagination onto the man – unconsciously. You create a certain aura around the man; he creates a certain aura around you. Everything seems to be beautiful because you are making it beautiful, because you are dreaming it, avoiding the reality. And you both are trying in every possible way not to disturb the other's imagination.

So the woman is behaving the way the man wants her to behave; the man is behaving the way the woman wants him to behave. But this you can do only for a few minutes or a few hours at the most. Once you get married and you have to live together twenty-four hours a day, it becomes a heavy burden to go on pretending something that you are not.

Just to fulfill the imagination of the man or the woman, how long can you go on acting? Sooner or later it becomes a burden, and you start taking revenge. You start destroying all that imagination that the man has created around you because you want not to be imprisoned in it; you want to be free and just be yourself.

And the same is the situation with the man: he wants to be free and just be himself. And this is the constant conflict between all lovers, all relations.

When you are sharing your joy, you don't create a prison for anybody: you simply give. You don't even expect gratitude or thankfulness, because you are giving not to get anything, not even gratitude. You are giving because you are so full, you have to give it.

So if anybody is thankful, you are thankful to the person who has accepted your love, who has accepted your gift. He has unburdened you, he has allowed you to shower on him.

And the more you share, and the more you give, the more you have. So it does not make you a miser, it does not create a new fear that, 'I may lose it.' In fact the more you lose it, the more fresh waters are flowing in from springs you have not been aware of before.

If the whole existence is one, and if the existence goes on taking care of trees, of animals, of mountains, of oceans from the smallest blade of grass to the biggest star then it will take care of you too.

Why be possessive? The possessiveness shows simply one thing that you can't trust existence. You have to arrange separate security for yourself, safety for yourself; you cannot trust existence.

Non-possessiveness is basically trust in existence.

There is no need to possess, because the whole is already ours.

Drop the idea that attachment and love are one thing. They are enemies. It is attachment that destroys all love.

If you feed, if you nourish attachment, love will be destroyed; if you feed and nourish love, attachment will fall away by itself.

Love and attachment are not one; they are two separate entities, and antagonistic to each other.

And always remember the basic rule of life: If you worship someone, one day you are going to take revenge.

You are to be aware not to be manipulated by anybody, howsoever good their intentions are. You have to save yourself from so many well-intentioned people, do-gooders, who are constantly advising you to be this, to be that. Listen to them and thank them. They don't mean any harm – but harm is what happens.

Just listen to your own heart.

That is your only teacher.

People have judged you, and you have accepted their idea without scrutiny. You are suffering from all kinds of people's judgments, and you are throwing those judgments on other people. This game has got out of all proportion, and the whole humanity is suffering from it.

If you want to get out of it, the first thing is: Don't judge yourself. Accept humbly your imperfection, your failures, your mistakes, your frailties. There is no need to pretend otherwise. Just be yourself, that, 'This is how I am full of fear. I cannot go in the dark night. I cannot go in the thick forest.' What is wrong in it? it is just human.

Once you accept yourself you will be able to accept others, because you will have a clear insight that they are suffering from the same disease. And your accepting them will help them to accept themselves.

We can reverse the whole process: you accept yourself; that makes you capable of accepting others. And because somebody accepts them, they learn the beauty of acceptance for the first time how peaceful it feels and they start accepting others.

If the whole humanity comes to point where everybody is accepted as he is, almost ninety percent of misery will simply disappear it has no foundations and your hearts will open of their own accord, your love will be flowing.

Truth is always pure, nude, alone. And there is a great beauty, because truth is the very essence of life, existence, nature.

Except man, nobody lies. A rosebush cannot lie. It has to produce roses; it cannot produce marigolds it cannot deceive. It is not possible for it to be otherwise than it is. Except man the whole existence lives in truth.

Truth is the religion of the whole existence – except man. And the moment a man also decides to become part of existence, truth becomes his religion.

And it is the greatest revolution that is possible to happen to anyone. It is the glorious moment.

You don't see the world as it is, you see it as your mind forces you to see it. And this you can see all over the world.

Different people are conditioned in different ways; and mind is nothing but conditioning. They see things according to their conditioning, that conditioning is a certain color.

We make distinctions; we make somebody superior, somebody inferior; man is more powerful, woman is less powerful; somebody is more intelligent, somebody is less. Races have been claiming they are the chosen people of God. Every religion is claiming that their book is written by God Himself. All these things, layer upon layer, make your mind.

Unless you are able to put the whole mind aside and see the world directly, immediately, with your consciousness, you will never be able to see the truth.

In this world the greatest courage is to put the mind aside. The bravest man is one who can see the world without the barrier of the mind, just as it is. It is tremendously different, utterly beautiful. There is nobody who is inferior and there is nobody who is superior there are no distinctions.

Ordinarily we think intellectuals are intelligent people. That is not true. Intellectuals live only on dead words. Intelligence cannot do that. Intelligence drops the word that is the corpse and just takes the living vibe from it.

The intelligent man's way is the way of the heart, because the heart is not interested in words; it is interested only in the juice that comes in the containers of the words. It does not collect containers, it simply drinks the juice and throws away the container.

To me, the religious man is not one who is above nature, but is one who is totally natural, fully natural, who has explored nature in all its dimensions, who has not left anything unexplored.

One has to live a natural life to attain a natural death. The natural death is the culmination of a life lived naturally, without any inhibition, without any depression just the way animals live, the birds live, the trees live; without any split a life of let-go, allowing nature to flow through you, without any obstructions from your side, as if you are absent and life is moving on its own.

Rather than you living life, life lives you; you are secondary. Then the culmination will be a natural death.

Death will reflect the ultimate culmination, the crescendo of your whole life. In a condensed form, it is all that you have lived.

So only very few people in the world have died naturally, because only very few people have lived naturally.

We are afraid of death because we know we are going to die, and we don't want to die. We want to keep our eyes closed. We want to live in a state as if 'everybody else is going to die, but not me.' That is the normal psychology of everybody: 'I am not going to die.'

To bring up death is taboo. People become afraid because it reminds them of their own death. They are so concerned with trivia, and death is coming; they want that trivia to keep them engaged. It functions as a curtain: they are not going to die, at least, not now, later on. 'Whenever it happens, we will see.'

Accepting life in its totality, you have accepted death too; that it is just a rest. The whole day you have been working, and in the night do you want to rest or not? The daily sleep rejuvenates you, makes you again capable of functioning better, efficiently. All tiredness is gone, you are again young.

Death does the same on a deeper level. It changes the body, because now the body cannot be rejuvenated by only ordinary sleep; it has become too old. It needs a more drastic change, it needs a new body. Your life energy wants a new form. Death is simply a sleep so that you can easily move into a new form.

A man living out of fear is always trembling inside. He is continuously on the point of going insane, because life is big, and if you are continuously fearful then there is every kind of fear.

You can make a big list and you will be surprised how many fears are there, and still you are alive! There are infections all around, diseases, dangers, kidnapping, terrorists and such a small life. And finally there is death, which you cannot avoid. Your whole life will become dark.

Drop the fear. The fear was taken up by you unconsciously in your childhood. Now consciously drop it and be mature. And then life can be a light which goes on deepening as you go on growing.

Responsibility is not a game. It is one of the most authentic ways of living dangerously. .

To me, disobedience is a great revolution. It does not mean saying an absolute no in every situation. It simply means deciding whether to do it or not, whether it is beneficial to do it or not. It is taking the responsibility on yourself.

Unless you know the truth of your being, you will never feel the great benediction of life. You will never be able to overflow with joy just for the sheer fact of existence.

If you cannot experience truth, you will not be able to connect yourself with this vast cosmos – which is your home. It has given birth to you, and it has the tremendous expectation of you that you will grow to the ultimate peak of consciousness, because through you existence can become conscious. There is no other way.

Intellect is thinking and consciousness is discovered in a state of no-thinking, so utterly silent that not even a single thought moves as a disturbance. In that silence you discover your very being it is as vast as the sky. And to know it is really to know something worthwhile; otherwise all your knowledge is garbage.

Your knowledge may be useful, utilitarian, but it is not going to help you transform your being. It cannot bring you to a fulfillment, to contentment, to enlightenment, to a point where you can say, 'I have come home.'

There is no home, unless we find it in ourselves.

Giving love is the real, beautiful experience, because then you are an emperor. Getting love is a very small experience, and it is the experience of a beggar.

Don't be a beggar. At least as far as love is concerned be an emperor, because love is an inexhaustible quality in you; you can go on giving as much as you like. Don't be worried that it will be exhausted, that one day you will suddenly find, 'My God! I don't have any love to give any more.'

Love is not a quantity, it is a quality, and a quality of a certain category that grows by giving, and dies if you hold it. If you are miserly about it, it dies. So be really spendthrift! Don't bother to whom. That is really the idea of a miserly mind that 'I will give love to certain persons with certain qualities.'

You don't understand that you have so much, you are a raincloud. The raincloud does not bother where it rains on the rocks, in the gardens, in the ocean it doesn't matter. It wants to unburden itself, and that unburdening is a tremendous relief.

So the first secret is: Don't ask for love.
Don't wait, thinking that you will give if
somebody asks you give it!

The most basic thing to remember is when you are feeling good, in a mood of ecstasy, don't start thinking that it is going to be your permanent state.

Live the moment joyfully, as cheerfully as possible, knowing perfectly well it has come and it will go just like a breeze comes into your house, with all its fragrance and freshness, and goes out from the other door.

If you start thinking in terms of making your ecstatic moments permanent, you have already started destroying them. When they come, be grateful; when they leave, be thankful to existence. Remain open. It will happen many times. Don't be judgmental, don't be a chooser, remain choiceless.

Yes, there will be moments when you will be miserable. So what? There are people who are miserable and who have not even know a single moment of ecstasy. You are fortunate.

Even in your misery, remember that is is not going to be permanent; it will also pass away. So don't get too disturbed by it. Remain at ease. Just like day and night, there are moments of joy and there are moments of sadness. Accept them as part of the duality of nature, as the very way things are.

And you are simply a watcher; neither you become happiness, nor do you become misery. Happiness comes and goes, misery comes and goes. One thing remains always there, always and always – and that is the watcher, one who witnesses.

M editation is concerned with the very essential core of your being, which cannot be divided into male and female.

Consciousness is simply consciousness.

A mirror is a mirror it is not male, it is not female it simply reflects. Consciousness is exactly like a mirror which reflects.

And meditation is allowing your mirror to reflect, simply to reflect the mind in action, the body in action. It doesn't matter if the body is a man's or a woman's; it does not matter how the mind functions emotionally or logically. Whatever the case, the consciousness has simply to be alert to it.

That alertness, that awareness, is meditation.

S lowly slowly get more and more centered in the watcher. Days will come and nights will come, lives will come and deaths will come, success will come, failure will come. But if you are centered in the watcher because that is the only reality in you, everything is a passing phenomenon.

Just for a moment, try to feel what I am saying: Just be a watcher. Do not cling to any moment because it is beautiful, and do not push away any moment because it is miserable. Stop doing that. That you have been doing for lives, and you have not been successful yet, and you will never be successful ever.

The only way to go beyond is to remain beyond, to find a place from where you can watch all these changing phenomena without getting identified.

Experience comes and goes don't rely on it. Unless you have found the experiencer who is feeling the joy, who is feeling pain, who is feeling well-being, who is feeling sad, who is this consciousness....

Every effort should be made to reach to this innermost center of the cyclone. Your whole life is a cyclone of change, of changing scenes, changing colors; but just in the middle of the cyclone there is a silent center. That is you.

Once you get identified with a certain idea, then you are sick. All identification is mental sickness.

In fact, mind is your sickness.

To put the mind aside and just to look silently without any thought, without any prejudice into reality, is a healthy way of being acquainted with reality. And you will find a totally different reality.

The finding of the real will release you from many stupidities, many superstitions. It will clean your heart of all kinds of rubbish that generations have poured into you. Diseases go on from generation to generation; you inherit the whole past with all its stupid ideas. Otherwise, there is no distinction, there is no comparison.

And once you are free from making comparisons and distinctions, you are light, your whole existence is light. You lose all heaviness. You become so light that you can open your wings and fly.

Everything passes, but you remain; you are the reality. Everything is just a dream – beautiful dreams are there, nightmares are there. But it does not matter whether it is a beautiful dream or a nightmare, what matters is the one who is seeing the dream.

That seer is the only reality.

The seer is something absolutely eternal.

Just a little glimpse of it and all your problems will start disappearing because a totally new perspective will arise, a new vision, a new way of life, a new way of seeing things, seeing people, responding to situation.

And the seer is always present, twenty-four hours a day: Whatever you are doing or not doing, it is there. It has been there for centuries, for eternity, waiting for you to take note of it. Perhaps because it has been always there, that's why you have forgotten it. The obvious is always forgotten remember it.

When you are feeling a well-being, a euphoria, remember it.

When you are in misery, in anguish, remember it.

In all climates, in all moods, go on remembering it. Soon you will be able to remain centered in it, there will be no need to remember. And that is the greatest day in one's life.

I say unto you, there is no evil and there are no evil forces in the world. There are only people of awareness, and there are people who are fast asleep and sleep has no force.

The whole energy is in the hands of the awakened people. And one awakened person can awaken the whole world. One lighted candle can make millions of candles lighted without losing its light.

Misery nourishes your ego that's why you see so many miserable people in the world. The basic, central point is the ego.

To understand love, first you should be loving; then only can you understand love. Millions of people are suffering: they want to be loved but they don't know how to love. And love cannot exist as a monologue; it is a dialogue, a very harmonious dialogue.

It is not what people give to you that satisfies, it is what you give to people that satisfies. It is not by being a beggar that you can be contented, it is by being an emperor. And love, when you give, makes you an emperor.

You can give so much, inexhaustibly, that the more you give, the more refined, the more cultured, the more perfumed your love becomes.

The moment you understand what love is you experience what love is you become love. Then there is no need in you to be loved, and there is no need in you that you should be loving: loving will be your simple, spontaneous existence, your very breathing. You cannot do anything else, you will be simply loving.

Now if, in return, love does not come to you, you will not feel hurt, for the simple reason that only the person who has become love can love. You can give only that which you have.

Asking people to love you people who don't have love in their life, who have not come to the source of their being, where love has its shrine...how can they love you? They can pretend. They can say they do. They can even believe they do. But sooner or later it is going to be known that it is only a pretension, that it is only acting, that it is hypocrisy.

There may not be an intention to deceive you, but what can the person do? You ask for love, and the other person also wants love. Both understand it that you are expected to love, only then can you get love so you both try in every possible way. It is a posture, but the posture is empty. Both are going to discover it, and both are going to complain about it against the other, that it is not right. From the very beginning it has been two beggars begging from each other, and both have only empty begging bowls.

Ego is the greatest bondage, the only hell that I know of.

Those who have found the source of love within themselves are no longer in need of being loved and they will be loved.

They will love for no other reason but simply they have too much of it just as a raincloud wants to rain, just as a flower wants to release its fragrance, with no desire to get anything. The reward of love is in loving, not in getting love.

And these are the mysteries of life, that if a person is rewarded just by loving people, many will love him, because by being in contact with him they will slowly start finding the source within themselves. Now they know one person at least who showers love, and whose love is not out of any need. And the more he shares and showers his love, the more it grows.

Don't think of the truth as an object it is not an object. It is not there, it is here.

Mind functions in an either/or way: either this can be right or its opposite can be right. Both together cannot be right as far as the mind, its logic, its rationality, is concerned.

If mind is either/or, then the heart is both-and.

The heart has no logic, but a sensitivity, a perceptivity. It can see that not only can both be together; in fact, they are not two. It is just one phenomenon seen from two different aspects.

And if there is a question of choosing between the mind and the heart, the heart is always right, because mind is a creation of the society. It has been educated. You have been given it by the society, not by existence.

The heart is unpolluted.

The heart is pure existence; hence it has a sensitivity.

Look from the viewpoint of the heart, and contradictions start melting like ice.

I say to you: To be one with the universe you have to disappear and let existence be. You just have to be absent so that existence can be present in its totality. But the person who I am saying has to disappear is not your reality, it is only your personality; it is just an idea in you.

In reality you are already one with existence. You cannot exist in any other way you are existence.

But the personality creates a deception, and makes you feel separate. You can assume yourself to be separate, existence gives you total freedom even being against itself. You can think yourself a separate entity, an ego. And that is the barrier that is holding you back from melting into the vastness that surrounds you every moment.

Looking at a sunset, just for a second you forget your separateness: you are the sunset. That is the moment when you feel the beauty of it. But the moment you say that it is a beautiful sunset, you are no longer feeling it; you have come back to your separate, enclosed entity of the ego. Now the mind is speaking.

And this is one of the mysteries, that the mind can speak, and knows nothing; and the heart knows everything, and cannot speak. Perhaps to know too much makes it difficult to speak; the mind knows so little, it is possible for it to speak. Language is enough for it, but is not enough for the heart.

But sometimes, under the impact of a certain moment a starry night, a sunrise, a beautiful flower just for a moment you forget that you are separate. And even forgetting it releases tremendous beauty and ecstasy.

In life nothing is permanent, nothing can be permanent. It is not within your hand to make anything permanent. Only dead things can be permanent. The more alive a thing is, the more fleeting.

Today love is there, tomorrow one knows not: it may be there, it may not be there. It is not in your hands to control it. It is a happening. You cannot do anything; you cannot create it if it is not there. Either it is there or it is not there you are simply helpless.

The stones may be permanent. The flowers cannot be.

And love is not a stone. It is a flower, and of a rare quality.

Heart is the transcendence of duality. Heart sees things clearly, and love is its natural quality nothing to be trained in. And this love has no hate as a counterpart.

You are capable of going beyond the love/hate duality. Right now they go on hand in hand in your life. You love the same person you hate, so in the morning it is hate, in the evening it is love – and it is a very confusing thing. You don't even understand whether you love the person or you hate the person, because you do both at different times.

But this is how the mind functions; it functions through contradictions. Evolution also functions through oppositions, but those oppositions in existence are not contradictions, they are complimentaries.

Hate is also a kind of love standing upside down.

Love that comes from the mind is always lovehate. It is not two words, it is one word: 'lovehate' not even a hyphen dividing them. And a love that comes from your heart is beyond all dualities....

Everyone is in search of that love that goes beyond love and hate but he is searching with the mind, and hence he is miserable. Every lover feels failure, deception, betrayal, but nobody is at fault. The reality is that you are using a wrong instrument. It is as if somebody is using eyes to listen to music, and then freaks out that there is no music. But eyes are not meant for listening, nor are ears meant to see.

Mind is a very businesslike, calculating mechanism; it has nothing to do with love.

Love will be a chaos, it will disturb everything in it. Heart has nothing to do with business it is always on holiday. It can love, and it can love without ever turning its love into hate; it has no poisons of hate.

Everybody is searching for it, but just through a wrong instrument; hence the failure in the world. And slowly slowly people, seeing that love only brings misery, become closed: 'Love is all nonsense.' They create a thick barrier against love. But they will miss all the joys of life, they will miss all that is valuable....

Friendship is the purest love. It is the highest form of love where nothing is asked for, no condition, where one simply enjoys giving. One gets much; but that is secondary, and that happens of its own accord.

To live without future is the greatest courage. Only cowards live in the future.

Man's past has been very cowardly. It was living, not in the present, but in the future:

'All that has to happen, is to happen tomorrow.' And in that hope people lived, and they died. What they were waiting for never turned up: it proved to be waiting for Godot.

The present has remained unexplored, unlived

– and that is the only reality there is.

Whatever you want your death to be, let first your life be exactly the same because death is not separate from life.

Death is not an end to life, but only a change.

Life continues, has continued, will always continue. But forms become useless, old, more a burden than a joy; then it is better to give life a new, fresh form.

Death is a blessing, it is not a curse.

The simplest method of meditation is just a way of witnessing. There are one hundred and twelve methods of meditation, but witnessing is an essential part of all one hundred and twelve methods. So as far as I am concerned, witnessing is the only method. Those one hundred and twelve methods are different applications of witnessing.

The essential core, the spirit of meditation, is to learn how to witness.

You are seeing a tree; you are there, the tree is there, but can't you find one thing more? – that you are seeing the tree, that there is a witness in you which is seeing you seeing the tree.

The world is not divided only into the object and the subject. There is also something beyond both and that beyond is meditation.

To be homeless is to be free, it is freedom. It means there is no attachment, no obsession with anything outside; that you are not in need of getting some warmth from the outside but your warmth is within you. You have the source of warmth; you don't need more. So wherever you are without a home, you are, strangely, at home.

The people who are searching for the home are always getting into despair, and finally are going to feel, 'We have been cheated, life has cheated us. Somehow it gave us the desire for finding a home and there is no home at all, it simply does not exist.'

We try to make a home in every possible way: one finds a husband, one finds a wife, one brings children into the world.... One tries to create a family that is a psychological home. One makes not just a house but tries to make it almost a living entity. A person tries to make a house according to his dreams, that it is going to be a fulfillment of warmth, that in this coldness....

And it is vast, the coldness of existence. The whole universe is so cold, so indifferent that you want to create a small shelter for yourself where you can feel that you are taken care of, that something protects you, that it is something that belongs to you, that you are an owner, not a homeless wanderer.

But in reality this kind of idea is going to create misery for you, because one day you will find the husband you have lived with, the wife you have lived with you are strangers. Even after living fifty years together, the strangeness has not disappeared; on the contrary, it has deepened. You were less strangers on the first day you had met.

As time has passed and you have been together, you have become more and more strangers, because you have come to know each other more and more and now you don't understand at all who the other person is. The more you have known, the less you know. It seems the more you have become acquainted with the person, the more you have become aware that your ignorance about the other is absolute; there is no way to destroy it.

Your children you have thought they are your children, and one day you find they are not your children. You have been just a passage they have come through. They have their own life they are absolutely strangers. They don't belong to you. They will find their own ways and their own life.

Who is with you?

Nobody is with anybody.

You are in a crowd always, but alone. Either alone or in the crowd makes no difference, either in the home or just a wanderer it makes no difference.

For the ego, aloneness is never a joy. Ego enjoys only when it subordinates somebody, when it can say, 'I am higher than you, bigger than you.'

Ego can never enjoy aloneness; in aloneness what is the point of having an ego?

Live and love, and love totally and intensely – but never against freedom. Freedom should remain the ultimate value.

We have been taught continually that love is a relationship, so we have become accustomed to that idea. But that is not true. That is the lowest kind, very polluted.

Love is a state of being.

Every time one realizes something of the truth, there is a dance in the heart. The heart is the only testimony for the truth.

And it cannot testify through words.

The heart can testify in its own way: through love, through dance, through playing music – non-verbal. It speaks, but it does not speak in language and logic.

Time is always uncertain. This is the difficulty with the mind: mind wants certainty – and time is always uncertain.

So when just by coincidence mind finds a small space of certainty, it feels settled; a kind of illusory permanence surrounds it. It tends to forget the real nature of existence and life; it starts living in a kind of dream world, which starts taking on the appearance of reality.

It feels good for the mind because mind is always afraid of change, for the simple reason, Who knows what change will bring? good or bad. One thing is certain, that the change will unsettle your world of illusions, expectations, dreams.

Mind is just like a child playing on the seashore, making palaces in the sand. For a moment it seems that the palace is ready but it is made of shifting sands. Any moment just a small breeze, and it will be shattered to pieces. But we start living in that dream palace. We start feeling that we have found something which is going to remain always with us.

But time continuously goes on disturbing the mind. It looks hard, but it is really very compassionate of existence to remain always with you. It does not allow you to make realities out of appearances. It does not give you a chance to accept masks as your real face, your original face.

People think that to remain unchanging in their principles gives them a certain strength. They are wrong. It simply sucks all their strength. They are the weakest people on the earth.

They are like small children who have grown up and are still using the pajamas which were made when they were babies. Now they are looking awkward, they are feeling some difficulty. They are holding their pajamas up all the time because they are slipping down again and again, and people are laughing.

No, as you grow, your pajamas also should grow. But because pajamas don't grow, you have to change them.

So I don't see any problem in it. But I can see this is not only one person's situation, millions of people are living this way. They make a strict discipline and then get into trouble. Nobody is putting this trouble onto them it is their own principles. If they leave them, they feel bad; if they follow them, they suffer.

I teach you clearly an unprincipled life, a life of intelligence which changes with every change around you, so you don't have a principle that creates a difficulty in changing. Be absolutely unprincipled and just follow life, and there will be no misery in your life.

We should be discontinuous with the past – it was completely sick. Man has lived a very sick life because he created a very sick philosophy, and he followed it very seriously.

We should be discontinuous with that sickness howsoever respectable and howsoever ancient and rediscover man's totality.

And that can be done only when we join playfulness with reverence; when playfulness becomes a deep reverence; when reverence does not lead you to die, to renounce, but leads you to rejoice, to dance, to celebrate.

Live like a warrior, this way or that, but never compromising. It is better to be defeated, but totally, than to be victorious through a compromise. That victory will not give you anything except humiliation; and the defeat without compromise will still give you dignity.

Life is mysterious: Here, sometimes victory is just shameful, and defeat is a dignity because one would not compromise.

Mind can only function with the expected, with the known. When there is something unexpected, unknown, then it has to stop. And the stopping of the mind is the sound of one hand clapping.

It is silence.

In a relationship, to be understanding means that you can be wrong, the woman may be right. It is not a guarantee that just by being a man you have the power and the authority to be right. Nor does the woman have that.

If we were just a little more human and a little more friendly, we could say to each other, 'I am sorry.' And what are the things you are fighting for? so small, so trivial that if somebody asks you, you will feel embarrassed.

Just drop the idea that everything has to fit; drop the idea that there is going to be total harmony because those are not good things. If everything fits you will get bored with each other. If everything is harmonious you will lose the whole juice of relationship.

It is good that things don't fit. It is good that there is always a gap so there is always something to explore, something to cross over, some bridge to be made.

Our whole lives can be a tremendous exploration of each other if we accept the differences, the basic uniqueness of each individual, and we don't make love a kind of slavery, but a friendship.

Who is going to teach you to sit silently? That is the most difficult thing in the world. You can do everything very easily, but the easiest thing to sit silently seems to be the most difficult.

Love has to be a friendly affair in which nobody is superior, in which nobody is going to decide about things; in which both are fully aware that they are different, that their approach towards life is different, that they think differently, and still with all these differences they love each other. Then you will not find any problems.

Problems are created by us.

Don't try to create something superhuman. Be human, and accept the other person's humanity with all the frailty humanity is prone to. The other will commit mistakes just as you commit mistakes – and you have to learn. To be together is a great learning in forgiving, in forgetting, in understanding that the other is as human as you are. Just a little forgiveness....

When people talk, they want to convert you to their opinion. It is trying to spread a subtle empire. When people talk, they want to indoctrinate you, because everybody who has a doctrine is deep down afraid about whether it is true or not.

The only way that he can feel that it is true is if he can indoctrinate many people and can see in their eyes conviction, conversion. Then he feels at ease, because the arithmetic is: 'If so many people are finding so much solace in what I am saying to them, then there must be something true in it.'

People are talking to others so that they themselves can believe in what they are saying.

Friendship can be of two types. One is friendship in which you are a beggar; you need something from the other to help your loneliness. The other person is also a beggar, he wants the same from you. And naturally, two beggars cannot help each other.

Soon they will see that their begging from a beggar has doubled or multiplied the need. Instead of being one beggar there, now there are two. And if unfortunately they have children, then it is a whole company of beggars who are asking and nobody has anything to give.

So everybody is frustrated and angry, and everybody feels cheated, deceived. And in fact nobody is cheating and nobody is deceiving, because what have you got to give?

The other kind of friendship, the other kind of love, has a totally different quality. It is not of need; it is out of having so much that you want to share. A new kind of joy has come into your being that of sharing which you were not ever aware of before, because you have always been begging.

When you share, there is no question of clinging.

You flow with existence, you flow with life's change, because it doesn't matter with whom you share. It can be the same person tomorrow, your whole life the same person, or it can be different persons.

It is not a contract, it is not a marriage; it is simply out of your fullness that you want to give. So whatsoever happens to be near to you, you give it. And giving is such a joy.

In the world of habits it is all repetition. In the world of consciousness there is no repetition.

Man is born homeless, and man remains his whole life homeless; man dies homeless. To accept this truth brings a tremendous transformation. Then you don't search for the home – because home is something there, far away, something other than you. And everybody is searching for a home. When you see the illusoriness of the home, then, rather than searching for the home, you will start searching for the being that is born homeless, whose destiny is homelessness.

There is no way to make a home.

And this is a miracle: the moment that you realize that there is no way to make a home, then this whole existence is home. Then wherever you are, you are at home.

In life, everything that is significant is absurd.

No intelligent person is interested in dominating others. His first interest is to know himself. So the highest quality of intelligence goes towards mysticism, and the most mediocre goes after power. That power can be worldly, political, it can be of money...it can be of holding spiritual domination over millions of people, but the basic urge is how to dominate more and more people.

This urge arises because you don't know yourself, and you don't want to know that you don't know yourself.

You are so afraid of becoming aware of the ignorance that prevails in the very center of your being, you escape from this darkness through these methods lust for money, lust for power, lust for respectability, honor. And a man who has darkness within himself can do anything destructive.

Creativity is impossible from such a person, because creativity comes from your being conscious, a little alert, having light, love. Creativity is not at all interested in dominating anyone for what? The other is the other. Neither you want to dominate anyone, nor do you want to be dominated by anyone. Freedom is the very taste of being just a little alert.

In trust, all that is beautiful in love is implied. 'Trust' is perhaps the most beautiful word in the human language. And trust is so close to truth that if it is total, then this very moment your trust becomes your truth, a revelation, a revolution.

Freedom is your flowering, your lotus opening in the morning sun. And unless that happens you cannot find contentment, fulfillment, a peace that one feels when one comes home.

And everybody is carrying his home within himself.

You are not to go anywhere; you have to stop going so that you can remain where you are, so that you can remain what you are.

Just be. And in that utter silence of being are hidden all the mysteries of existence.

Don't search for the home, because there is none.
Search for yourself, because there is one!

Love helps you to reach to the place where trust is possible. Without love, trust is not possible. Love is almost like a bridge, which can collapse any moment, but still it is a bridge. If you can use it, it can take you to trust, but without it, you cannot reach to trust directly.

So love is a necessity, but unto itself, not enough. Its use is as a means; the end is the trust.

In trust, all that is beautiful in love is implied. 'Trust' is perhaps the most beautiful word in human language. And trust is so close to truth that if it is total, then this very moment your trust becomes your truth, a revelation, a revolution.

The moment you trust in let-go, the moment you stop struggling against existence, then you need not worry about anything. Existence takes care.

The whole trouble with the human mind is that it is constantly fighting, it is trying to go against the current. There is a reason why it does so: only going against the current does it fill the ego. Just going with the flow of life, without any struggle, letting life lead you wherever it wants to, your ego will disappear.

You will be, you will be more than you are now – more authentic, more true but there will be no sense of 'I.' And then you will be able to see where you are going.

Even the path that is created as you move can be seen by those who have no egos. You can even see the footprints of the birds flying in the sky. They don't make any footprints. But when the mind is clear of the ego, the whole being becomes such a clean mirror that even those footprints reflect in it.

One thing I know: Existence has no goal, and as part of existence I cannot have any goal.

The moment you have a goal, you cut yourself off from existence. Then a small dewdrop is trying to fight against the ocean. Unnecessary is the trouble, meaningless is the struggle.

Love is beautiful, but changing. It is beautiful, but cannot be relied upon. Today it is there, tomorrow it is gone. Love is more juicy than trust, more natural than trust, but trust is a higher quality.

In the dictionaries 'trust' is almost misrepresented; it means trusting someone who is trustworthy; it is more objective because the man is trustworthy, you trust him. It is not your quality; it is the quality of the other person upon whom your trust depends. And because there are rarely trustworthy people around, millions of people have forgotten what trust is, there is no chance for it. A trustworthy person is needed, and there are no trustworthy persons anywhere.

Nobody trusts anybody; hence 'trust' has become a dry word, inexperienced just a word, with no juice, with no taste.

When I use the word 'trust,' it is totally different: I don't mean you trust somebody who is trustworthy. That is not trust. The man is trustworthy so it is not a credit to you. When I say 'trust,' I say trust in spite of the man, in spite of whether he is trustworthy or not. In fact when he is not trustworthy, then to trust...then only will you find for the first time something new arising in your consciousness. And then trust will become a very lighted phenomenon, far more superior than love, because it needs nothing from the other.

Only an independent, totally autonomous being, living in freedom, can attain to the experience of truth.

Trust is not competitive; hence there is no jealousy. You can trust me; millions of people can trust me. In fact the more people trust me, the more happy you will be. You will be rejoicing that so many people are trusting. Not so with love.

When you say, 'I love you,' there is a subtle current of possessiveness. Without being said, it is understood that, 'Now you are my possession nobody else should love you.'

In trust there is no question of possessing the person you trust. On the contrary, you are saying, 'Please possess me. Destroy me as an ego. Help me to disappear and melt in you so there is no resistance going with you.'

Love is a constant struggle, a fight.

Love demands.

'I love you,' means, 'You have to love me too. In fact I love you only because I want you to love me.' It is a simple bargain; hence the fear that, 'You should not love anybody else, nobody else should love you, because I don't want anybody to be partners in my love, to be sharers in my love.'

The unconscious mind of man goes on thinking as if love is a quantity, that there is a certain quantity of love: 'If I love you, then you should possess the whole quantity. If I love a few other people, then the quantity will be distributed; you will not be getting the whole of it.

Hence the jealousy, the spying, the fighting, the nagging all that is ugly goes on behind a beautiful word, 'love.'

In trust there is no question of any fighting. It is really a surrender. When you say, 'I trust in you,' it means, 'From this moment my fight with you stops. Now I am yours.'

Trust is certainly a higher value than love. In trust, love is implied, but in love, trust is not implied. When you say, 'I trust in you,' it is understood that you love.

But when you say you love, trust has nothing to do with it. In fact your love is very suspicious, very untrusting, very much afraid, always on guard, watching the person you love. Lovers become almost detectives. They are spying on each other.

Love is beautiful if it comes as a part of trust because trust cannot be without love.

Rather than going after the sought, search for the seeker. And finding the seeker, you suddenly find that the whole existence is your home; so wherever you are, you are at home.

Just finding yourself, you find that the whole existence is your home.

It is true that when you say, 'I love you,' it is not a surrender, it is not a readiness to be dissolved. It is not a readiness to be taken to unknown and unknowable spaces. When you say, 'I love you,' you stand equal, and there is a certain aggressive equality in it.

But when you say, 'I trust you,' it is a deep surrender, an openness, a receptivity, a declaration to yourself and to the universe that, 'Now if this man takes me even to hell, it is okay with me. I trust him. If it looks like hell to me, it must be my fault of vision. He cannot take me to hell.'

In trust you will always find faults with yourself.

In love you will always find faults with the one you are in love with.

In trust you are always, without saying it, in a state of apology that, 'I am ignorant, I am sleepy, unconscious. There is a possibility of saying something wrong, doing something wrong, so be merciful towards me, have compassion towards me.'

Trust implies so much. It is such a treasure.

The world of 'more' is the world of the ordinary man. The world of not going after more, not after any goal ahead of you, but just looking in the moment where you are, who you are, and taking a plunge into the presentness of your consciousness this is the only revolution, and the only religion, and the only spirituality there is.

This earth is one, single whole. We should be proud that our planet in this vast universe, where there are millions of solar systems having millions and millions of planets.... Our planet is the only one which has evolved, not only life, not only consciousness, but has even produced the ultimate flowering of consciousness in people like Gautam the Buddha, Lao Tzu, Tilopa, and many more.

We should be proud of this planet earth.

Only a choiceless person squeezes the juice of life to its totality. He is never miserable. Whatever happens he finds a way to enjoy it.

And this is the whole art of life to find a way to enjoy it. But the basic condition has to be remembered: Be choiceless. You can be choiceless only if you are alert, aware, watchful; otherwise you are going to fall into choice.

Life certainly is an art, the greatest art – and the shortest formula is choiceless awareness, applicable to all situations, all problems.

When I say that except man everything is living truth the ocean, the clouds, the stars, the stones, the flowers that everything is nothing but truthfulness, nothing but just itself, with no mask, that only man is capable of deceiving others, of deceiving himself it has to be remembered that this is a great opportunity. It has not to be condemned, it has to be praised, because even if a rosebush or a lotus wants to lie, it cannot. Its truth is not freedom, its truth is a bondage. It cannot go beyond its boundaries.

Man has the prerogative, the privilege of being untrue. That means man has the freedom to choose. If he chooses to be truthful, he is not choosing bondage, he is choosing truth and freedom. Freedom is his privilege. In the whole existence, nobody else has freedom. But there are dangers when you have opportunities.

When you have freedom, you can go wrong.

No rose can go wrong, no rock can go wrong. You can go wrong; hence a deep awareness of each act, of each thought, of each feeling, has to penetrate you.

Only man needs to seek truth; everything else has already got it, but the glory of freedom is not there. You have to seek it and find it; and in that very seeking and finding, you are glorious, you are the very crown of existence.

Misery is nothing but choice. You choose the experience of love, the feeling of ecstasy, but by choosing you are going to be caught in a natural process. You will cling to these feelings and they are not permanent; they are part of a wheel which is moving.

Just like the day and the night: if we choose the day, what can you do to avoid the night? The night will come. The night does not bring misery, it's your choice of the day against the night which is creating misery.

Every choice is bound to end up in a miserable state.

Choicelessness is blissfulness.

And choicelessness is let-go.

It means the day comes, the night comes, the success comes, the failure comes, the days of glory come, the days of condemnation come and because you have not chosen anything, whatever comes is alright with you, it is always fine with you.

Slowly slowly you will see a distance growing in you: the circle will go on moving but you are not caught in it. It doesn't matter to you whether it is day or night. You are centered in yourself; you are not clinging to something else, you are not making your center somewhere else.

The whole question is if you can live without any choice. Whatever comes, enjoy it. When it goes, then something else comes, enjoy it. Day is beautiful, but night is beautiful in its own way why not enjoy both. And you can enjoy both only if you are not attached to one.

Once you accept life in its totality life includes death then death is not against life but is just a servant, just as sleep is. Your life is eternal it is going to be there forever and forever but the body is not eternal; it has to be changed. It becomes old, and then it is better to have a new body, a new form, rather than dragging along in the old.

To me, a man of understanding will not have any problems. He will have only a clarity to see – and the problems evaporate. Tremendous silence is left behind, a silence of great beauty and great benediction.

Truth is the greatest offender.

Borrowed knowledge is ignorance. Experienced truth makes you not knowledgeable, but humble. The more you know it, the less you claim to know it. The day you know it perfectly, you can only say, 'I am in utter ignorance; I am just a child, collecting sea shells on the beach. I know nothing.'

'I do not know' can only be said by a man who knows perfectly.

The people who say 'We know' are utterly ignorant people, but their memories are full. But those memories are dead because they have not given birth to any experience of their own.

To me, to be natural is to be spiritual. My effort is to create the natural man human, with no guilt, accepting all the frailties, failures, the human being is prone to.

In this deep acceptance of your natural being is the seed of your transformation.

We have made our lives full of mundane things, mundane acts, because we don't know a simple secret that can transform the quality of everything that we do.

And remember, if you don't know the secret of transformation, amongst those mundane things you are also mundane unless you have a consciousness which makes you sacred and holy, which is going to transform everything that you do into the same category in which you are.

Then whatever you touch will become sacred.

Whatever you do will become holy.

Nature is not anguish, it is blissfulness. It is not anxiety, misery, suffering. It is love, it is rejoicing. It is a constant celebration.

We come out of this nature, we are part of this nature we inherit the same qualities in our consciousness.

When you feel existence immediately – without any mediator, with no mind given by anybody else to you you taste something which transforms you, which makes you enlightened, awakened, which brings you to the highest peak of consciousness.

A greater fulfillment there is not. A higher contentment there is not. A deeper relaxation there is not. You have come home.

Life becomes a joy, a song, a dance, a celebration and I call this life, religious.

A man is needed who is brought up without any religious belief system, without any political ideology. His education is only a sharpening of the intelligence so that one day he can find his own truth.

And remember, if the truth is not your own, it is not truth. To be truth it has to be your own, your own experience you cannot borrow it.

Anything of beauty, anything reminding you of the beyond, will create a longing in you, a longing you cannot figure out for what. You don't know the name of the object because in fact it is not for any object.

Listening to beautiful music, watching a sunset or just a bird on the wing or beautiful roses, or sitting in silence, a sweet pain can be felt.

The longing is how to become one with this state of feeling so that it should not be a fleeting thing that comes and goes, but something that remains with you, that becomes you.

The same music which was sweet today may not be sweet tomorrow, may be boring the day after tomorrow. So it is not the music, it is something else that is triggered in you the longing to be peaceful, to be musical, to have all the beauty of existence, and to have it forever.

It is a spiritual longing, a longing for the beyond, beyond all fleeting experiences; a longing to stop time and be here now, in this moment eternally.

This is true religiousness.

God can die, religions can disappear, but religiousness is something interwoven into existence itself. It is the beauty of the sunrise, it is the beauty of a bird on the wing. It is the beauty of an opening lotus. It is all that is truthful, all that is sincere and authentic, all that is loving and compassionate.

Religiousness includes everything that pulls you upwards, that does not make you stop where you are, but keeps always reminding you that you have yet far to go. Every place that you stop for a rest is only a rest for the night; in the morning we go again on the pilgrimage. And it is an eternal pilgrimage.

I want everyone to become an existential gypsy. You don't need roots you are not trees.

You are human beings.

Trust simply means that whatever happens we are with it, joyously. Not reluctantly, not unwillingly then you miss the whole point but dancingly, with a song, with a laughter, with love.

Whatever happens is for the good. Existence cannot go wrong. If it does not fulfill our desires, that simply means our desires were wrong.

Man's greatest need is to be needed. If somebody needs you, you feel gratified. But if the whole existence needs you, then there is no limit to your bliss. And this existence needs even a small blade of grass as much as the biggest star; there is no question of inequality.

Nobody can substitute for you. If you are not there, then existence will be something less and will remain always something less it will never be full. That feeling that this whole, immense existence is in need of you takes all miseries away from you.

For the first time, you have come home.

Evolution is trying, through humanity, to reach to the ultimate peak of consciousness. A few people have reached; they are proof enough that everybody can reach just a little effort, just a little sincerity, just a little search.

Everything is telling you that the way you are living is not enough, the things that you are doing is not all; that your mundane life is only of the superficial your real life remains, in most cases, untouched. People are born, they live and they die, and without knowing who they are.

The whole existence is silent. If you can also be silent, you will know who this consciousness is within you. And knowing this, life becomes a joy, a moment-to-moment rejoicing, an unending festival of lights.

The real prayer is only one, and that is to live in such a way that you start feeling grateful towards existence. Existence has given you such an opportunity which you had never asked for, which you never deserved, and yet you got it. And you blossomed into thousands of flowers, and you left the world with the fragrance of thankfulness.

Act more consciously, and you will be coming closer and closer to a quality that can only be called godliness not God, not a person, but a quality, a fragrance.

Act unconsciously, and you will be coming closer and closer to something which cannot be personified as the devil but can only be called a quality evilness.

The unconscious mind behaves in wrong ways; the conscious mind behaves in right ways.

And the only religion there is, is the art of changing the unconscious mind into consciousness, so that you don't have the duality of conscious and unconscious, but you have only one a pure light, a pure consciousness.

And out of that consciousness, everything is divine.

Always be ready to move from the known to the unknown in anything, any experience. It is better, even if the unknown proves worse than the known that is not the point. Just your change from the known to the unknown, your readiness to move from the known to the unknown, is what matters. It is immensely valuable.

Always remember that the new is better than the old.

I say that even if all that is old is gold, forget about it. Choose the new gold or not gold, it doesn't matter. What matters is your choice: your choice to learn, your choice to experience, your choice to go into the dark.

Meditation is the only answer to all the questions of man. It may be frustration, it may be depression, it may be sadness, it may be meaninglessness, it may be anguish; the problems may be many, but the answer in one.

Meditation is the answer.

There have been attempts all over the world to make a harmonious human society, but all have failed for the simple reason that nobody has bothered about why it is not harmonious naturally.

It is not harmonious because each individual inside is divided, and his divisions are projected in the society. And unless we dissolve the individual's inner divisions, there is no possibility of really realizing a utopia and creating a harmonious society in the world.

So the only way for a utopia is that your consciousness should grow more, and your unconsciousness should grow less, so finally a moment comes in your life when there is nothing left which in unconscious: you are simply a pure consciousness. Then there is no division.

Naturally, in the world, action is needed, not inaction. For every success action is needed, not inaction. For all ambitions, action is needed. So the whole world by and by has become focused on the active part.

But the active part is going to create tensions; it is going to create anguish, sadness. Even if you achieve your goal, you will find that you have not achieved anything you simply wasted your time and your energy.

The active part of your mind cannot leave you in a state of silence, relaxation, just at ease, at home. That is impossible for the active mind.

It is the inactive mind that can give you a home to rest in, a shelter, and a beautiful feeling that nothing has to be done; that you are good as you are, that you are at the goal already, so you have not even to move.

The world can come to a harmony if meditation is spread far and wide, and people are brought to one consciousness with themselves. This will be a totally different dimension to work with.

Up to now it was revolution. The point was society, its structure. It has failed again and again in different ways. Now it should be the individual; and not revolution, but meditation, transformation.

And it is not so difficult as people think. It is only a question of understanding the value of meditation

Then it is easily possible for millions of people to become undivided within themselves. They will be the first group of humanity to become harmonious.

And their harmoniousness, their beauty, their compassion, their love all their qualities are bound to resound around the world.

Humanity is in danger every moment. By the end of this century, if we have survived it will be a miracle.

This is something fundamental to realize, that truth can only be your own experience. There is no other way to get it.

Lies you can get in abundance all kinds of lies, all colors, all shapes and sizes, whichever you prefer. They are available and suitable to you. You do not have to fit with them, they fit with you. It is very easy; they are made for you, they are tailored for you.

Truth is a totally different matter.

You will have to fit with it. Truth knows no compromise. You will have to change according to it you will have to go through a transformation.

A man with a religious mind will be religious in his actions, relations, in his thoughts, feelings. He does not need a church or synagogue or a temple. What he needs is a clarity of vision, a silence of the heart, an experience of his own being because his experience of his own being will make him aware that the whole world is divine; that everything that exists is at different stages of evolution, but there is in it the potential of life and the potential of consciousness.

Mind does not know three tenses. It knows only two: past and future. Present is non-existential to the mind: The existential is non-existential to the mind; and the non-existentials are existential to the mind.

Hence the whole effort is how to get out of the mind, how to get out of the non-existentials and to stand in the middle where existence is.

How to be in the present? that is the whole knack of meditation. And the moment you are in the present, enlightenment is its by-product.

Humanity is in danger every moment. By the end of this century, if we have survived it will be a miracle.

All the arts have their origin in meditation; and all the arts have moved far away from meditation and this is a calamity. Otherwise every artist, whatever his special art, should find a way towards meditation. But it doesn't seem to be so.

On the contrary, most of the modern artists, musicians, dancers, poets, painters, sculptors, rather than reaching to meditation, end up in madness that is the other extreme of meditation. And the reason is because in the original sources the gaps were important, not the words. But as time passed words became more important than the gaps.

No man who has been meditative has ever committed suicide, has ever gone mad, for the simple reason that he is going towards more balance, towards more inner harmony, and finally towards absolute harmony that is the harmony of no-mind.

And to attain to no-mind is to attain all.

There is nothing more than that, because it is peace, it is silence, it is blissfulness.

No-mind is godliness, it is immortality, it is eternity.

Western psychology is still wandering around the roots. It has not even touched the foliage, the flowers, the fruits. There is no question of it going into no-mind; it has not even been able to take note of the whole mind. And without knowing the whole mind you cannot jump into the no-mind.

No-mind is realization.

No-mind is enlightenment.

No-mind is liberation.

Scientists will never be able to understand the abysmal depth, the darkness, and the mysterious part of their own minds.

If there is only one science, there can be only one religion. If one science is enough to explore the objective world, one religion is enough to explore the inner world of men; and that one religion need not have any adjective to it – Christian, Hindu, Taoist, or anything.

Just as science is simply science, religion is simply religion.

In fact, according to me, there is only science, with two dimensions: one dimension working on the outside world, the other dimension working on the inside world. We can even get rid of the word 'religion.'

This is a fundamental rule of science, that a minimum of hypotheses should be used. So why use two words? just one word is enough. And

'science' is a beautiful word; it means

'knowing.'

Knowing the other is one aspect, knowing one's self is another aspect; but 'knowing' covers both.

If you are ready to open a new door into your being, if you are ready to hear from the heart, then whatever I am saying is so simple that there is no need to believe in it because there is no way to disbelieve in it. It is so simple that there is no way to doubt it.

Hence I am against belief for the simple reason that for all my teaching, no belief is needed. I am all for doubt because for my simple teaching, you cannot doubt.

Our conditionings don't allow us to be natural. Our conditionings from the very beginning teach us that we have to be something more than nature, that just to be natural is to be animal we have to be supernatural.

And it seems very logical. All the religions have been teaching this that to be man means going above nature. And they have convinced centuries of humanity to go above nature.

Nobody has succeeded in going above nature. All that they have succeeded in doing is destroying their natural, spontaneous beauty, their innocence.

I would like to tell you that only one thing decides a true master, and that is that his presence can make your dormant mind suddenly alive; it can put you on fire. It can make you blossom into thousands of flowers, just in a single moment. The moment becomes so intense that it is almost equal to eternity. This is the only way to decide everything else is meaningless.

Two persons thinking, are two; two persons non-thinking, are one because there is no distinction, no boundary both are in the same state.

Thoughts will be different, will draw a boundary of separation. But no-thought has no boundary and no distinctions, no differences.

Two innocent beings are one.

When a mature person becomes a child again...there is a difference between the ordinary children and the reborn. The ordinary child is innocent because he is ignorant; and the reborn innocence is the greatest value in life because it is not ignorance, it is pure intelligence.

Innocence alone becomes ignorance.

Intelligence alone becomes cunningness.

Both together they are neither ignorance nor cunningness, but simply a receptivity, an openness...a heart which is capable of wondering at the smallest thing in life.

And the man who knows the feeling of wonder, to me, is the only religious man. It is through his wonder that he comes to know that existence is not just matter, it cannot be. This is not a logical conclusion for him, not a belief for him but a real experience. Such a beautiful experience so mysterious, so unfathomable indicates tremendous intelligence in it.

But existence is not cunning. It is very simple, it is innocent.

So if one can keep these two qualities – innocence and intelligence together, one needs nothing else. These two will lead one to the ultimate goal of self-realization.

Mind sees things in black and white – nothing in between. Day and night, nothing in between. Life and death, nothing in between. Love and hate, nothing in between.

Mind simply divides, splits, cuts a thing into two separate, polar realities, makes them so contradictory that it seems impossible that there could be a way that they are not separate, that they could be one reality.

The mind has taken only the two ends of one reality. That's how it is. Logically, love and hate are opposites, contradictory, but existentially that's not true. Love can move easily into hate without any barrier. Hate can move into love just like waves moving into other waves with no barriers anywhere.

It is our idea that light and dark are two, contradictory realities. That's not true. There is no opposition. At the most we can say the light is less dark, and darkness is less light. But we have to use something which makes only a difference of degrees and does not create any contradiction.

And we see every day life moving into death so calmly, so quietly, without making any fuss. You cannot even hear the footsteps of death. There cannot be any contradiction. And those who know, know the other side also that death that goes on moving into new forms of life. All distinctions are man-made existence is distinctionless.

Once we start thinking of a distinctionless, one reality not dividing into dualities, dichotomies the cross from our mind can disappear. Nobody else has crucified you; you are yourself responsible, because you can put the cross away from you and your whole mind can become one.

Thoughts are substitutes for awareness.

This is something to be remembered, that whenever you experience something of which there is no opposite, you have come home.

While the opposite exists you will be torn apart continuously. Between these two experiences you will be just a football sometimes feeling happy, sometimes feeling miserable, but never knowing yourself that there is something beyond both the beautiful and the depressive. That's why it cannot be brought into words, because all words are dualistic; otherwise they won't have any meaning.

That is the nature of language: you cannot have a word without having its opposite. If you don't have the opposite, then the word won't have any meaning.

The nameless phenomenon to which total trust leads is not a relationship. It is at-onement. The two disappear...it has become one circle, one pole. And it always comes without any pre-information, just suddenly, like a breeze. But once you have tasted it that love and trust all seem to be very poor you have known richness. It may have been only for a few seconds, it does not matter.

Love is not very reliable, but useful.

Use it, and move to trust.

But trust is also not a hundred percent proof.

Move beyond.

Then you cannot fall; then there is no way of going back. Then it is something which partakes of eternity.

To experience this moment is, at the same time, to experience all that has been and all that will be, because this moment contains both.

It contains the whole past, because where will the past go? It goes on and on entering into the present moment. And it contains the whole future, because from where will the future come? It will grow from this moment, the next moment and the next moment, and the whole eternity.

The present moment is a seed which has all the trees of the past, generations and generations of trees. This seed has not come from nowhere, it has come from a tree. That tree had come from another seed, that seed had come from another tree. If you go backwards the seed will take you to the very beginnings if there were any beginnings. It has been forever here.

And this seed also contains the future trees. From this seed will grow a new tree, and that tree will grow thousands of seeds and thousands of trees. A single seed can make the whole earth green; or it can even be said, it can make the whole universe green so much is contained in a small seed.

Beyond love and trust is a space which is neither objective nor subjective, which is simply there.

There are many things in existence which cannot be named, and those are the real things. That which can be named is of a lower quality, of a lower stratum.

That unnamed, silent space...it contains love, it contains trust, and plus. And the 'plus' is so vast. But it can only come, you cannot drag it.

The present moment is a seed of time. It is invisible that's why we don't know what it contains. It contains the whole past; it contains the whole future.

That's why I insist: Don't think of the past, don't think of the future. Just remain in the present moment, and the whole past is your and the whole future is yours.

The unknown is always continuously entering into your known world and disturbing it. But it disturbs it only because you don't welcome it. If you can welcome the unknown, and you can leave the known....

It is always the known that is disturbed by time it is not the unknown. The unknown cannot be disturbed by time or by anything.

If you are ready to welcome the unknown, you know the secret of remaining victorious in all the defeats and all the failures.

Darkness has a silence and darkness has a depth. Darkness has peace, and darkness takes away all your knowledge, takes away everything that you thought belonged to you. It leads you absolutely into the unknown and into the mysterious.

To me, darkness is one of the greatest mysteries in existence far greater than light.

Those who are afraid of darkness will never be able to enter into their own being. They will go round and round, they will never reach themselves.

And it has to be darkness, not light, because light comes and goes; once you have discovered the spot of darkness in you, you have discovered something that is eternal, something indestructible, something which is more than what you know of life. It is the basic substance existence is made of.

A koan is a puzzle which cannot be solved; there is no way to solve it. It is a strategy to tire your active mind so much so that out of tiredness it falls flat; it recognizes its failure.

In those moments the focus can be moved very easily. Because mind has failed, you can move towards no-mind.

It was for a certain reason that mystics called meditation 'no-mind,' because if you call it meditation, again the mind makes a goal out of it. Then you have to achieve meditation. So it makes no difference whether the goal was enlightenment or meditation; the goal remains, the future remains, and goes on destroying the present.

The mystics who for the first time changed from 'meditation' to 'no-mind' had a tremendous insight. Now no-mind cannot be made a goal. Mind cannot make it a goal. It is simply absurd how can mind make a goal of no-mind? It will simply say it is not possible, mind is all, there is no no-mind.

This was a strategy not to allow you to make it a goal. Very few people have understood the strategy, that that's why they have called it no-mind to prevent the mind from making it a goal.

So be more and more in a state of no-mind.

Just go on removing memories, imagination, to clean and clear the present moment. And as it deepens, as you become more and more capable of having no-mind, enlightenment comes of its own accord.

Just the way love functions as a means to trust, trust also functions as a means to something beyond for which no word exists in any language. It is an experience. It is not a question of love, not a question of trust, but something absolutely unknown to the mind.

Love and trust help you to reach to it.

So remember, they are only means to an end for which no name exists.

But suddenly, when trust is total, you may have a glimpse of it.

It is overpowering; you simply disappear.

Truth cannot be said, so whatever can be said is going to be a beautiful lie beautiful because it can lead towards truth.

So I make a demarcation between lies: beautiful lies and ugly lies, ugly lies which take you away from truth, and beautiful lies which take you close towards truth. But as far as their quality is concerned, they both are lies.

But those beautiful lies work; hence in some way they partake of the flavor of truth.

The real juice of life is within you. This very moment you can turn within yourself, look into yourself. No worship is needed, no prayer is needed. All that is needed is a silent journey to your own being.

I call it meditation, a silent pilgrimage to your own being.

And the moment you find your own center, you have found the center of the whole existence.

The extremist is always an egoist.

At certain moments you are more aware; at certain moments, less aware.
So it is possible to create the situation for being more aware.

That's why awareness became the basis of meditation. And with awareness
came the surprise that as you become aware, thoughts disappear. When you
are fully aware, there are no thoughts, and suddenly, time has stopped.

How can you arrive at a natural death living an unnatural life?

Death is others' opinion about you.

Only an awakened man can die a natural death;
otherwise all deaths are unnatural, because
all lives are unnatural.

Death is simply the culmination point, the crescendo of your life.
It is not against life, it does not destroy life.

To die beautifully, one has to live beautifully.

To die amazingly and in excitement, in ecstasy, one has to prepare
one's whole life for ecstasy, excitement, amazement.

When I say you have to disappear for the realization of the ultimate, I do not mean you; I mean the you that you are not. I mean the you that you think you are.

The you that you realize when you are one with the existence is not the old you. That was your personality and this is your individuality. That was given by society, and this is nature, reality, a gift of existence.

Two persons thinking, are two; two persons non-thinking, are one because there is no distinction, no boundary both are in the same state.

Thoughts will be different, will draw a boundary of separation. But no-thought has no boundary and no distinctions, no differences.

Two innocent beings are one.

Truth is not an object that you will find somewhere when you are silent. Truth is your subjectivity.

Just try to understand. You are there, and the world is there: whatever you see is an object, but who is seeing it is the subject. In silence, all objects disappear you have the whole infinity, and just silence. It is full of consciousness, it is full of presence, it is full of your being. But you will not find anything as the truth. That will become an object – and truth is never an abject.

Truth is subjectivity.

To discover your subjectivity unhindered, unobjected by anything in its total infinity and eternity, is the truth.

Witnessing is finding your inside mirror. And once you have found it, miracles start happening.

When you are simply witnessing your thoughts, thoughts disappear. Then there is suddenly a tremendous silence which you have never known. When you are watching your moods anger, sadness, happiness they suddenly disappear and an even greater silence is experienced.

And when there is nothing to watch, then the revolution: then the witnessing energy turns upon itself because there is nothing to prevent it, there is no object left.

The word 'object' is beautiful. It simply means that which prevents you, 'objects' you. When there is no object to your witnessing, it simply comes round back to yourself to the source, and this is the point where one becomes enlightened.

Enlightenment is simply recognizing your being, recognizing the eternity of your being, recognizing that there has been no death before, nor is there any death again that death is a fiction.

Seeing your being in its utter nakedness, in its absolute beauty, its grandeur, its silence, its blissfulness, its ecstasy all that is involved in the word 'enlightenment.'

Once you have experienced that juice, mind starts losing its grip on you because you have found something which is qualitatively so high, so fulfilling, such a tremendous contentment, that mind feels its function is finished.

The mind looks ugly because it has only given you misery, worries, anxiety. What has been its contribution to you? Its grip loosens; it starts hiding in shadows, and by and by it falls away.

You continue to live, but now your living is moment to moment; and what you have got as a by-product in that small gap of no-mind goes on growing. There is no end to that growth.

Enlightenment only begins, it never ends.

I am not trying to give you any ideals that you have to become this or that. I am simply trying to help you to see that you are already that which you need to be.

Just drop all longing, all desire, all ambition to be someone else, so that you can be just whatever you are.

I don't want to distract you from your being. I want to come closer and closer to your being so finally only you are left within yourself.

Desire as such is always unspiritual. So there cannot be any spiritual desire.

Man is existence's greatest experiment. In this vast, infinite universe, only on this small earth has existence been able to produce humanity which has the potential to become totally conscious.

Existence expects much from you.

For more information:

www.OSHO.com
a comprehensive multi-language website including a magazine, OSHO Books, OSHO TALKS in audio and video formats, the OSHO Library text archive in English and Hindi and extensive information about OSHO Meditations. You will also find the program schedule of the OSHO Multiversity and information about the OSHO International Meditation Resort.

To contact OSHO International Foundation visit: www.osho.com/oshointernational

About the Author
Osho's teachings defy categorization, covering everything from the individual quest for meaning to the most urgent social and political issues facing society today. His books are not written but are transcribed from audio and video recordings of extemporaneous talks given to international audiences over a period of 35 years. Osho has been described by the Sunday Times in London as one of the "1000 Makers of the 20th Century" and by American author Tom Robbins as "the most dangerous man since Jesus Christ."

About his own work Osho has said that he is helping to create the conditions for the birth of a new kind of human being. He has often characterized this new human being as "Zorba the Buddha"—capable both of enjoying the earthy pleasures of a Zorba the Greek and the silent serenity of a Gautam Buddha. Running like a thread through all aspects of Osho's work is a vision that encompasses both the timeless wisdom of the East and the highest potential of Western science and technology.

Osho is also known for his revolutionary contribution to the science of inner transformation, with an approach to meditation that acknowledges the accelerated pace of contemporary life. His unique "Active Meditations" are designed to first release the accumulated stresses of body and mind, so that it is easier to experience the thought-free and relaxed state of meditation.

Two autobiographical works by the author are available:
Autobiography of a Spiritually Incorrect Mystic by Osho, St. Martin's Griffin (2001) ISBN: 978-0312280710
Glimpses of a Golden Childhood by Osho The Rebel Publishing House ISBN: 8172610726

Osho International Meditation Resort
The OSHO International Meditation Resort is a great place for holidays and a place where people can have a direct personal experience of a new way of living with more alertness, relaxation, and fun. Located about 100 miles southeast of Mumbai in Pune, India, the resort offers a variety of programs to thousands of people who visit each year from more than 100 countries around the world. Originally developed as a summer retreat for Maharajas and wealthy British colonialists, Pune is now a thriving modern city that is home to a number of universities and high-tech industries. The Meditation Resort spreads over 40 acres in a tree-lined suburb known as Koregaon Park. The resort campus provides accommodation for a limited number of guests, in a new 'Guesthouse' and there is a plentiful variety of nearby hotels and private apartments available for stays of a few days up to several months.

Meditation Resort programs are all based in the Osho vision of a qualitatively new kind of human being who is able both to participate creatively in everyday life and to relax into silence and meditation. Most programs take place in modern, air-conditioned facilities and include a variety of individual sessions, courses and workshops covering everything from creative arts to holistic health treatments, personal transformation and therapy, esoteric sciences, the "Zen" approach to sports and recreation, relationship issues, and significant life transitions for men and women. Individual sessions and group workshops are offered throughout the year, alongside a full daily schedule of meditations. Outdoor cafes and restaurants within the resort grounds serve both traditional Indian fare and a choice of international dishes, all made with organically grown vegetables from the resort's own farm. The campus has its own private supply of safe, filtered water. www.osho.com/resort.